RURAL AGEING

A good place to grow old?

Edited by Norah Keating

For Ruth and Bill Keating

First published in Great Britain in 2008 by

The Policy Press
University of Bristol
Fourth Floor
Beacon House
Queen's Road
Bristol BS8 1QU
UK

Tel +44 (0)117 331 4054
Fax +44 (0)117 331 4093
e-mail tpp-info@bristol.ac.uk
www.policypress.org.uk

British Library Cataloguing in Publication Data
A catalogue record for this book is available from the British Library.

Library of Congress Cataloging-in-Publication Data
A catalog record for this book has been requested.

ISBN 978 1 86134 901 9 paperback
ISBN 978 1 86134 902 6 hardcover

Cover design by In-Text Design, Bristol
Front cover: photograph kindly supplied by Getty Images
Printed and bound in Great Britain by Henry Ling Ltd, Dorchester

Contents

Foreword by Alexandre Kalache iv

Acknowledgements vi

Notes on contributors viii

one A critical human ecology perspective on rural ageing 1
   Norah Keating and Judith Phillips

two Crossing borders: lifecourse, rural ageing and disability 11
   Tamara Daly and Gordon Grant

three Rurality and ageing well: 'a long time here' 21
   Sherry Ann Chapman and Sheila Peace

four The evolution of networks of rural older adults 33
   G. Clare Wenger and Norah Keating

five Distance, privacy and independence: rural homecare 43
   Joanie Sims-Gould and Anne Martin-Matthews

six Respite for rural and remote caregivers 53
   Neena L. Chappell, Bonnie Schroeder and Michelle Gibbens

seven Ageing, disability and participation 63
   Janet Fast and Jenny de Jong Gierveld

eight Participation in rural contexts: community matters 75
   Julia Rozanova, Donna Dosman and Jenny de Jong Gierveld

nine Staying connected: issues of mobility of older rural adults 87
   Bonnie Dobbs and Laurel Strain

ten Ageing and social exclusion in rural communities 97
   Thomas Scharf and Bernadette Bartlam

eleven Age-friendly rural communities 109
   Jacquie Eales, Janice Keefe and Norah Keating

twelve Revisiting rural ageing 121
   Norah Keating

References 131

Index 151

Foreword

Population ageing is a major force shaping the 21st century. The number of people aged 60 years and over as a proportion of the global population will double from 11% in 2006 to 22% by 2050. By then, there will be more older people than children for the first time in human history. While Europe, North America and Oceania are the oldest regions of the world – and will remain so in upcoming decades – developing countries are ageing faster within a context of scarcer resources. Population ageing marks the culmination of successful human development during the last century and presents major challenges for this century. Living longer is the fruit of critical gains in public health and in standards of living. The World Health Organization (WHO) recognises the importance of this demographic trend as expressed in its 1996 Brasilia Declaration on Ageing that 'healthy older people are a resource for their families, their communities and the economy'.

While older adults may be an important resource, they do not always live in settings in which they are able to flourish. And those in rural communities may be doubly disadvantaged. Like others, they require supportive and enabling living environments to compensate for physical and social changes associated with ageing. While some may live in idyllic settings, buffered from the social problems of urban areas, many face challenges of poor service infrastructure, isolation, poverty and harsh climate. They need to be assisted and protected.

Rural communities benefit a country's entire population. They produce food and other basic necessities of daily living, provide natural resources that underpin national industries and often help to preserve the environment. Yet to be sustainable, rural communities must provide the structures and services to support their residents' well-being and productivity. *Rural ageing* provides an in-depth critical analysis of ways to ensure that rural settings are places in which older adults can flourish, as well as identifying barriers that can lead to exclusion.

In this book, authors speak to the connections of older adults to rural places and how identities of older adults are created and re-created in interaction with the landscapes that are integral to their lives. They also consider ageing in the context of important people in the lives of adults as they reach very old age and the challenges in providing services to older rural adults in widely dispersed communities and in supporting caregivers. Furthermore, the authors address questions of how communities foster social engagement and connections and undertake critical analyses of community-level influences on inclusion and support of older adults. They cast light on the varied, and often hidden, nature of disadvantage experienced by older rural residents as well as how community settings may create contexts that are 'age-friendly' and inclusive.

In recent years, WHO has been engaged in a global project to enhance community capacity to act as a resource for older adults. Focused on cities, the age-friendly approach encourages active ageing by optimising opportunities for health, participation and security to enhance quality of life as people age and to tap the potential that older people represent for their societies. *Rural ageing* provides the groundwork for expanding the scope beyond cities, spreading it to the many small and dispersed communities where so many older people worldwide live their lives.

Population ageing is the demographic imperative of the 21st century. It will impinge on all aspects of society, offering multiple opportunities but also immense challenges. History will judge countries according to their capacity to respond to those challenges with resolve and imagination. Those who succeed will reap the benefits and will be at the forefront of the demographic revolution. For that, good ideas, research and policies are all critical, which is what this book offers. Above all, it also expresses in varied and complementary ways, what is ever so important as individuals and communities age: the emphasis has to shift, from disablement to enablement. I salute the authors for their vision and hope that readers worldwide will feel as inspired as I have from reading this book.

Alexandre Kalache, Director, Ageing and Life Course Programme
World Health Organization

Acknowledgements

The process of moving a book from ideas to publication is complex and requires a great deal of skill on the part of many people. Judith Phillips, the Ageing and the Lifecourse series editor, provided ongoing encouragement, advice and mentorship along the way. Her input invariably was insightful and supportive. We met in tea shops and faculty offices and talked over long walks on both sides of the Atlantic. She was the touchstone over the two years of the process.

Chapters in the book were written by scholars in Europe and North America and reflect a number of research programmes and projects. Data for Chapters Three, Five, Seven, Eight, Nine and Eleven were drawn in part from a programme of research entitled 'Caring Contexts of Rural Seniors', funded by Veterans Affairs Canada (VAC) 2002-06. Special thanks to David Pedlar, Head of the VAC Research Directorate, for his unfailing support for our rural research. Chapter Three also draws on research funded by the Economic and Social Research Council (ESRC) (UK) where the 'Environment and Identity in Later Life' study formed part of the Growing Older Programme. Research for Chapter Nine had additional support from Health Canada; writing of this chapter was supported by a New Emerging Team grant, the Institute of Aging and the Rural and Northern Health Research Initiative, Canadian Institutes of Health Research.

The research on which Chapter Four is based was funded by the UK Department of Health through the Welsh Office and the ESRC 1978-99. Chapter Five was supported in part through postdoctoral funding to the first author from a Canadian Institutes of Health Research grant to the Nexus Home Care Project. Data for Chapter Six were drawn from the Care Renewal Project funded by The J.W. McConnell Family Foundation (Canada). Chapters Seven and Eight were drawn from two projects in a programme of research entitled 'Hidden Costs, Invisible Contributions: The Marginalization of "Dependent" Adults', funded by the Social Sciences and Humanities Research Council (SSHRC) (Canada) under its Major Collaborative Research Initiative 2001-07.

Quantitative analyses for Chapter Eight were conducted at the Research Data Centre (RDC) at the University of Alberta, Canada. The RDC is funded by SSHRC, Canadian Institutes of Health Research, the Canadian Foundation for Innovation and Statistics Canada. RDC provides access for researchers to analytic datasets from Statistics Canada national surveys. The Commission for Rural Communities (an operating division of the Countryside Agency) (UK) supported the empirical study on which Chapter Ten is based.

We are grateful to these funders for their assistance in developing the information for our critical examination of rural ageing. We also wish to thank the SSHRC for funding that supported workshops to develop the outline and approach to the book. My thanks to the authors for their perseverance in writing, revising and polishing their chapters. Their work forms the heart of the book.

The staff at The Policy Press provided practical and timely advice and input on editing and production. They assisted with the intricacies of book cover designs, pre-publication brochures, author biographies and style manuals. Special thanks to Emily Watt, Associate Commissioning Editor, who worked with me on details of the contract and reminded me of timelines; Jacqueline Lawless, Marketing Manager, who helped with the information for the book jacket and promotional flyers; Dave Worth, Production Manager, for discussions on the design of the book cover; and Alison Shaw, Director. I have been in good hands throughout.

A wonderful group of people at the University of Alberta were the keepers and archivists of the knowledge created for the book. Kara Leigh Jameson set up a superb web-based filing system; Agnes Pieracci edited chapters; Julia Rozanova conducted background literature searches; and Jacquie Eales managed the process of tracking and organising the many iterations of chapters.

Finally, to my husband Norm Looney, for his support and encouragement and for sharing with me the beautiful rural setting of Summerland, British Columbia where the final phases of the book were completed.

I am grateful to all of you.

Norah Keating

Notes on contributors

Bernadette Bartlam is Lecturer in Social Gerontology and Course Director of the MSc in Geriatric Medicine at Keele University, UK. Her research interests centre on ageing from a lifecourse perspective, and specifically on poverty and social exclusion of older people, new models of housing and social care, and health and wellbeing in later life.

Sherry Ann Chapman is a research associate with the Community–University Partnership for the Study of Children, Youth, and Families at the University of Alberta, Canada. With a PhD in Human Ecology and a Master's degree in Museum Studies, she has a well-developed understanding of the research world and also a practice background. Her research interests include: ageing-well theorising; material culture as applied to gerontology; ageing in rural Canada; qualitative research; and community-based research mentorship.

Neena Chappell is a Canada Research Chair in Social Gerontology and Professor at the Centre on Aging and the Department of Sociology at the University of Victoria, Canada. She is a Professor of the Royal Society of Canada, advising professor at East China Normal University in Shanghai, and distinguished visiting scholar at the University of Hong Kong. For 30 years she has been researching caregiving to and among older adults including filial piety among Chinese families, healthcare including care for those living with dementia, and healthcare policy for an ageing society. Her ninth book, *Health and Health Care in Canada: A Sociological View*, Don Mills, Ontario: Oxford University Press, is due out in September 2008.

Tamara Daly is an assistant professor with the School of Health Policy and Management at York University, Canada. Her research interests focus on gender and health, healthcare work, the comparative political economy of health, gender and critical disability, and the role of healthcare non-profits. Her current funded research projects investigate changes to the organisation and delivery of women's health services in Toronto, health restructuring in the long-term care sector, and the support needs and resources available to women living with HIV.

Bonnie Dobbs is Director of Research, Division of Care of the Elderly, and Associate Professor in the Department of Family Medicine at the University of Alberta, Canada. Her primary research interests include the effects of medical conditions on driving competence, the development of procedures for the identification of medically at-risk drivers, the consequences of driving cessation for medically impaired older drivers and their families, the role of support groups for individuals who have had to stop driving, and for their caregivers, to reduce the emotional and mobility consequences for those drivers and their families, and the role of transportation in maintaining the mobility and independence of older drivers in both rural and urban settings.

Donna Dosman is an adjunct professor with the Department of Human Ecology at the University of Alberta, and a regional manager with the Research Data Centre Program, Statistics Canada. Her research interests include the costs of providing care to older adults who are frail and persons with disabilities, family and friend care networks, and the contributions that older adults and persons with disabilities make to their community.

Jacquie Eales is a research manager with the Research on Aging, Policies, and Practice Research team in the Department of Human Ecology at the University of Alberta, Canada. Having grown up in a rural farming community in northern British Columbia, she is particularly interested in the interface between older adults and the rural communities in which they reside and the process of creating a best person–environment fit.

Janet Fast is a professor in the Department of Human Ecology at the University of Alberta, Canada. As a family economist, her research interests focus on the consequences of recent health and social policy reform for family and friends who care for frail older people and other adults with chronic illness and disability. Of particular interest are the economic consequences of having to accommodate employment to care demands. She is also exploring the social participation of older adults and adults with chronic illness and disability as it contributes to their own well-being and to broader society.

Michelle Gibbens is a research associate with the Winnipeg Regional Health Authority Research and Evaluation Unit in Winnipeg MB Canada. She has explored the meaning and experience of respite for unpaid caregivers through her work with the Multiple Sclerosis Society of Canada and VON Canada on the Care Renewal: Reaching Out to Caregivers initiative. Her research interests include unpaid caregiver support, knowledge translation, and evaluation research.

Jenny de Jong Gierveld is Professor Emeritus in the Faculty of Social Sciences, VU University in Amsterdam and Honorary Fellow of the Netherlands Interdisciplinary Demographic Institute in The Hague. Her research has addressed issues around social participation in partner relationships, living arrangements and social networks. A particular focus has been on loneliness and the construction of a loneliness scale.

Gordon Grant is Research Professor in the Centre for Health and Social Care Research, Sheffield Hallam University, UK. His research interests are the identity constructions of vulnerable groups and caregivers, family caregiving across the lifecourse, and inclusive research. Gordon's latest book, *User participation in health and social care research: Voices, values and evaluation* (2007), co-edited with colleagues from the UK and Sweden, has just been published by McGraw Hill Education and the Open University Press.

Norah Keating is a professor in the Department of Human Ecology at the University of Alberta, Canada. She is a social gerontologist with a longstanding interest in older adults in rural areas and is the author of *Aging in rural Canada* (1991) Toronto: Butterworths. Professor Keating is co-director of a multidisciplinary research team that does research on caregiving and social engagement/social isolation of older adults. She is involved in international research on ageing and sits on the executive of the International Association of Gerontology and Geriatrics.

Janice Keefe is Professor of Family Studies and Gerontology and Director of the Nova Scotia Centre on Aging at Mount Saint Vincent University, Canada. She holds a Canada Research Chair in Aging and Caregiving Policy and the Lena Isabel Jodrey Chair in Gerontology. Her research areas focus on older adults living in rural areas, continuing care policy and caregiving, including work and elder care, caregiver assessment and compensation, and human resource issues in home care.

Anne Martin-Matthews is Scientific Director of the National Institute of Aging of the Canadian Institutes of Health Research, and a professor in the Department of Sociology at The University of British Columbia, Canada. Her publications include two books, three edited volumes, and over 125 papers on ageing and health, intergenerational relations, social support, caregiving, work–family balance, and rural ageing. She is a Fellow of the Gerontological Society of America and of the Canadian Academy of Health Sciences.

Sheila Peace is Professor of Social Gerontology and Associate Dean (Research) in the Faculty of Health and Social Care at the Open University, UK. She is a member of the university's Centre for Ageing and Biographical Studies (CABS). She has longstanding interests in the field of environment and ageing, long-term care for older people, the context of care across the lifespan, and the regulation of social care services for older people.

Judith Phillips is Professor of Social Work and Gerontology at Swansea University, UK, and Director of the Wales Older People and Ageing Research and Development Network. Her research interests are in ageing and the environment, family and kinship networks, care work, social work, and social care and older offenders.

Julia Rozanova is a PhD candidate in the Department of Sociology of the University of Alberta, Canada, and is actively involved with the International Sociological Association as a Board Member of Research Committee 10 on Participation, Organizational Democracy, and Self-management. Her current research focuses on social participation of older adults, ageism, and representation of older people and their issues in the media. She has a longstanding interest in social justice and political economy.

Thomas Scharf is Professor of Social Gerontology and Director of the Centre for Social Gerontology at Keele University, UK. In recent years, his research has addressed issues around poverty and social exclusion of older people, and cross-national comparisons of ageing. A particular focus has been on the experience of ageing in both urban and rural environments.

Bonnie Schroeder has been the Caregiver Project Manager at VON Canada since 2000. Bonnie manages several caregiving-related projects at VON Canada under the themes of ageing, caregiving, employment, and policy. She is actively involved in the Ontario Association of Social Workers (OASW), and at present is a member of its Social Work in Gerontology Steering Committee. She is interested in caregiver support, education and respite as well as building capacity in communities to support caregivers.

Joanie Sims-Gould is a post-doctoral research fellow jointly funded by the Nexus Home Care Project (The University of British Columbia, Canada) and the Social and Economic Dimensions of an Aging Population project (McMaster University, Canada). Her research interests include caregiving, episodic crises and acute caregiving, the informal/formal care interface, intergenerational relations, end-of-life care, social work practice with older adults, and ageing in rural environments.

Laurel Strain is Director of the Alberta Centre on Aging, and a professor in the Department of Sociology, Faculty of Arts, at the University of Alberta, Canada. Her research interests focus on older adults' health, informal support/caregiving, and the use of formal health services, from a social science perspective.

Clare Wenger is Emeritus Professor of Social Gerontology at Bangor University, North Wales. Coming from a background in anthropology she has a continuing interest in the way in which older people create meaning and supportive structure in their lives in both developed and developing countries and in the context of migration.

ONE

A critical human ecology perspective on rural ageing

Norah Keating and Judith Phillips

Introduction

The purpose of this chapter is to establish and describe the critical human ecology lens that challenges assumptions about growing older in rural areas. This lens is an essential element of the book in which we consider the interactions of older adults with the rural contexts that shape their experiences. Rural communities incorporate many elements of diversity that influence the lives of older adults: climate, landscape, distance from family networks, availability and access to services, migration patterns, community economic viability, age, gender roles and relationships. In this chapter we establish the structure and overall approach to the book, presenting the overall goals of the book and how the chapters address these goals. Throughout, we address the question: 'Are rural communities good places to grow old?'.

Considering the 'rural' in rural ageing

The title of this book, *Rural ageing*, reflects our guiding assumption that experiences of ageing are diverse, and that understanding this diversity requires an expanded consideration of ageing in various contexts. Rural is one such context. As Bonnie Dobbs and Laurel Strain note in Chapter Nine, a substantial proportion of the world's population lives in rural areas – from approximately 25% in North and South America to more than 60% in Africa and Asia. Older adults are over-represented in these rural places and their proportion of the population is growing faster than in urban areas (Hart et al, 2005; Statistics Canada, 2007a).

Increasing importance is attached to the geographies of rural areas (Cloke et al, 1997; Friedland, 2002), challenging views of hinterlands bereft of opportunity and socially and culturally lagging (Wiebe, 2001) or of idyllic pastoral settings (Bell, 1997). Such unidimensional views of rurality leave little scope for understanding the variety of rural places. Furthermore, older adults have often been made invisible by 'predominantly male, white, middle class, middle-aged, straight and able-bodied' views of rural residents (Cloke et al, 1997, p 211). We expand these rural discourses through our focus on the lives of a variety of older adults in diverse rural surroundings.

There are a number of ways in which one can understand rurality, and definitions have been the subject of much debate. However, they can be broadly categorised within two approaches. These are rural as a distinctive type of locality and rural as a social representation (Halfacree, 1993; Atkin, 2003). Each provides a distinctive rural lens; each is useful for our purposes in understanding different elements of the lives of older adults.

Type of locality approaches distinguish rural places by virtue of defining their sociospatial characteristics. Commonly used elements of these approaches are population size, density and distance from larger/urban centres (Hart et al, 2005). Such approaches are useful because from this perspective rural communities are physically situated and can be described objectively. The size and dispersion of rural populations are important when it comes to thinking about the ways in which rural residents confront issues of distance. The physicality of rural settings also presents challenges in developing sound social and health policy and delivering services to small, dispersed communities. Speaking of rural Australia, Bourke et al (2004) note problems of reduced access to services due to distance, cost and lack of specialists in remote and low-density rural communities.

Such 'situated' definitions of rural can be problematic since they are not standard across countries. For example, in the UK, rural areas comprise villages, hamlets, isolated dwellings or remote small towns with fewer than 10,000 people (Barham and Begum, 2006). In contrast, in Canada the criterion for rural populations is fewer than 1,000 people (Statistics Canada, 2007b). There, remote communities take on a very different meaning where 'fly-in' communities with no road access are extreme examples of how physical isolation can make service delivery extraordinarily difficult. Despite their usefulness, such approaches have been criticised because they are atheoretical, without any assumptions about how these geographic features might structure rural life. Halfacree (1993) argues that they describe rural rather than define it. Yet governments around the world use such approaches to understanding rural. For example, the UK definition of rural is used as a platform for ensuring that organisations working with rural residents accurately represent their views, for monitoring change and for expanding the rural evidence base to inform policy development and influence key decisions (Commission for Rural Communities, 2007a, p 8).

Sociocultural approaches define rural as a social construct. They are less tangible than descriptive/geographic definitions, focusing on rural as a reflection of a set of attitudes, behaviours and beliefs. Rural people are typified as having a slower, less pressured way of life, strong community feeling, close connections to the land and conservative, traditional values (Atkin, 2003). Further, there is evidence that people living in the countryside believe that their lives differ from those who live in the city (Cloke et al, 1997). However, there have been relatively few comparative studies that have focused on the experiences of ageing of older rural residents (Giarchi, 2006a). Critical analyses of the ways in which rural areas differ with regard to whether they are experienced as inclusive of older adults have begun to address the experiences of rural (Giarchi, 2006a). In their study of rural exclusion in Britain, Scharf and Bartlam (2006a) document the lives of those older adults who are excluded from full engagement in their communities because of poverty and social isolation.

One approach to enhancing understanding of social constructions of rural has been to explore how people understand and articulate their experiences in relation to their social and physical environments. Such contextual approaches are holistic, capturing both tangible and intangible aspects of locality in conceptualisations of rural (Williams and Cutchin, 2002). They have the advantage of incorporating elements of setting inherent in 'type of locality' definitions of rural. Yet they avoid the problem of the 'ecological fallacy' in which an inference about an individual is based on an aggregate of the group (Muilu and Rusanan, 2004). There are no assumptions of universal rural settings or persons from this perspective where diversity among rural people in rural settings is the focus, exemplified by the exploration of the various relationships between the attitudes, needs and values of older rural adults and the community settings in which they live.

Critical human ecology: key assumptions and concepts

Throughout the book we use a critical human ecology approach to understand rural adults in the environments in which they live and to critically evaluate their interactions with these environments. This lens was developed by drawing on two main bodies of theoretical literature: ecological/environmental literature from within the human ecology tradition, and critical gerontology. In this section we present key human ecology assumptions about contexts in which people live and describe the main contexts or environments of older rural adults.

Human ecology assumptions

Human ecology is a framework that is focused on the contexts in which people live their lives. Its main premise is that people do not exist in isolation but in interaction with the physical and social contexts in which they live (Bubolz and Sontag, 1993). Interactions among people and their contexts are dynamic. Human ecology is 'concerned with the processes and conditions that govern the lifelong course of human development in the actual environments in which human beings live' (Bronfenbrenner, 1994, p 1643) Throughout the book we describe rural contexts in North America and Europe, and the variety of experiences of adults living there.

A second premise of human ecology theory is that boundaries between environments are permeable so that characteristics of one environment interact with and influence others (Bubolz and Sontag, 1993). For example, physical characteristics of a rural community such as population size and distance from a larger centre may affect the availability of formal services. In turn, service availability may influence patterns of support among family and friend networks of older adults. Wahl and Lang (2004) argue that although researchers acknowledge the importance of interactions among contexts, they rarely address these interactions. Views of homogeneity of rural people and settings may arise in part from our lack of focus on the interface.

A third premise is that older adults are not passive recipients of the environments in which they live, but have varying capacities to make choices and to act on or adapt their environments (Marshall, 1999). Both personal and environmental resources influence the amount of 'agency' of older adults in rural settings. Those with higher levels of personal resources may be more able to manage even in resource-poor environments. For example, older people with good health and adequate income can travel to services unavailable in their communities. In contrast, those with limited health and financial resources may be able to manage only if they live in a community with good services or with a close-knit network of local family who can purchase or organise services on their behalf. The interface between personal and environmental resources has been called person–environment fit, a central idea in this framework (Scheidt and Norris-Baker, 2004).

Environments of older rural adults

Consistent with the human ecology assumption that individuals must be understood in context, we argue that one cannot fully understand whether rural areas are good places to grow old without taking into account the processes and interactions of older adults with their relevant environments. Environments are surroundings that 'encompass the person and affect their understanding of themselves and the culture in which they live' (Peace et al, 2006, p 8).

Environments are more or less immediate to the individual. They range from microenvironments that include face-to-face interactions with physical, familial and social aspects of a person's immediate surroundings (Bronfenbrenner, 1994) to macroenvironments that are regional, national or international (Bubolz and Sontag, 1993; Peace et al, 2006). In this book, we focus on those environments that help us deconstruct the assumptions described above: the macroenvironments of community and policy, and the more immediate physical and social microenvironments of older rural adults. From the human ecology perspective, 'a good place to grow old' is a place in which there is a good person–environment fit.

The physical environment includes the home and objects in the home, the built environment of buildings, roads and other amenities, and the natural environment including climate and topography. It includes both objective elements and the meaning or evaluation of those elements (Lawton, 1999; Peace et al, 2006). Stereotypes of rural communities are that they have relatively impoverished built environments with poor-quality housing and service amenities. In northern countries, climate is viewed as a barrier to rural living for older adults, exacerbating challenges presented by distance from service centres (Hanlon and Halseth, 2005).

The interpersonal environment includes one's connections to people with whom an individual has a personal relationship (Lawton, 1999). It includes networks of family members, friends and neighbours who can be a source of social capital that helps people interact with and navigate their surroundings (Peace et al, 2006). Social connections are important sources of support given and received and are fundamental to personal identity and well-being in later life (Rubenstein and de Medeiros, 2004). In contrast to beliefs about a poor physical environment, rural communities are often viewed as rich in people resources where older adults are embedded in strong networks of family and friends. Yet research findings suggest that this view of the interpersonal environment is more unidimensional than is warranted. For example, a report by Statistics Canada (2005a) showed that differences between Canada's urban and rural residents are smaller than they are often perceived to be in terms of various aspects of social engagement, isolation from family and friends or helping others.

There are many definitions of community and thus of community environment. Much of the focus of this book is on communities as physical places defined by structural characteristics such as population and distance that are seen as significant in structuring the lives of residents (Kendig, 2003). Scheidt and Norris-Baker (2004) have argued that the better that older persons know their immediate (community) environment, the more autonomy they can have, especially if they have limited personal resources. Thus, the longer that older persons have lived in their homes, the more likely they are to know about neighbourhood and community resources and to connect with others such as neighbours. Even those who are quite frail may create places in their homes where they have access to telephones and can see the neighbourhood, thus maintaining some community connection despite high levels of disability.

The policy environment is a macroenvironment that represents the values, programmes and services that affect rural older people. The policy environment has been described as a megasocial environment that includes norms and values as well as laws, programmes and regulations (Lawton, 1999). These broad values and the programmes that flow from them influence the service environment in rural areas. Programmes developed with assumptions that services can only be delivered efficiently in areas of high population density and short distances between centres will disadvantage many rural communities. Similarly, views of rural residents as resilient and resourceful can be used to drive policy agendas. An example comes from Alston (2007), who says that the Australian governments have responded to widespread drought that has exacerbated rural poverty by drawing on this assumption. Across the country they have introduced policy initiatives that champion the value of self-reliance among citizens. The result for rural Australia has been a withdrawal of services at a time of increased need.

Adding the critical gerontology perspective

Some approaches under the human ecology perspective have been criticised for being too descriptive, neglecting a critical analysis of the ways in which contexts provide opportunities and constraints to individuals living in various settings. To counterbalance this, we take an explicit critical perspective, marrying critical gerontology with the human ecology approach. We describe the main approaches of critical gerontology and how these approaches can be used to better understand contexts of rural older adults.

The origins of a critical approach come from a concern with a power differential within society that marginalised older people (Phillipson and Walker, 1986). Since its early development, critical gerontology has encapsulated a number of theories: political economy, social constructionist, feminist and, more recently, a focus on human rights as defining characteristics of a critical approach (Townsend, 2007). It is only recently that critical gerontology has engaged with environmental contexts in exposing the inequalities among older people in different geographical settings (Phillipson et al, 2000; Andrews and Phillips, 2005; Scharf et al, 2005a; Peace et al, 2006).

While the main focus of human ecology is on the contexts of people's lives, the main focus of critical gerontology is on the deconstruction of traditional concepts of ageing – the 'received wisdom'. Critical gerontology challenges conventional concerns and analyses (Achenbaum, 1997), such as the assumption that older people pose a burden on society and that distance and low population density mean that those in rural areas are particularly problematic. It moves beyond the usual concentration in gerontology on health and social care issues to environmental contexts in which people live as a basis for analysis (Andrews and Phillips, 2005). Conventional approaches look at what is wrong with environments (Joseph and Cloutier-Fisher, 2005) and what can be done to correct or adapt them to the needs of older adults, rather than to their ability to shape their environments and contribute positively to them. Critical approaches take seriously the idea that adults have agency when it comes to environmental interactions; older people can change, adapt and reconstruct their environments in which they live.

A critical perspective raises vital issues about the context of ageing. We need to look at older people within the context of their social, political, cultural and geographical environments, environments that potentially can disempower them. Ageism is challenged under a critical perspective both on a societal and individual level. For the most part, ageism has been seen as universal, devoid of a particular environmental context. Yet we have begun to consider ageism from a contextual perspective. For example, Laws (1997) talks about how space and place can marginalise people as they age. She describes how spaces may be inhabited and utilised in ways that exclude older people. Places or locations may also be inaccessible to them through poor design or lack of basic services – longstanding concerns in many rural communities. Similarly, as younger generations leave rural areas older people lose social capital and consequently are often further discriminated against.

Critical gerontology attempts to make the voices of marginalised groups heard. This poses a considerable challenge in engaging with people facing the 'double jeopardy' (Norman, 1985) of being isolated because of age and geography (remote locations), particularly for those who have difficult personal circumstances such as disability and dementia. Being in marginal geographical areas on the periphery can reinforce stigma and disadvantage.

Yet disempowerment of older adults is not taken for granted. Postmodern critical approaches also stress that people's lifestyles now are more varied than ever before (Phillips, 1996). The homogeneity of age – that all older people are the same – is challenged under critical gerontology. People differ in their resources and their ways of interacting with their environments. Older people in rural areas are different from each other and from rural older people in other environmental contexts. Environmental contexts also are diverse and incorporate cultural as well as spatial difference and diversity. This places importance on understanding the meaning of ageing in rural areas for older adults. The simple binary of urban–rural cannot be sustained in a discussion of environment and ageing in rural contexts.

Like human ecology, a critical perspective embraces ageing as a lifecourse issue. Phillips (1999) argues that conventional life stages now are less defined and that ageing and old age should be considered more appropriately as a fundamental part of entire human existence. A critical human ecology approach would argue that lives lived in rural areas evolve over time in interaction with specific contexts. There is no singular experience of old age in a rural setting. Critical gerontology in this context raises issues of the meaning of living in rural settings.

Policy and practice are challenged under a critical perspective. Policies that underpin the ageing experience and their effectiveness need to be examined and the evidence on which they have evolved explored. The narratives and biographies of older people need to be valued within this context and incorporated into policy praxis. Sense of place of older adults will shape and be shaped by their environmental location. The spatial dimensions of ageing have been neglected in social policy terms (Bernard and Phillips, 1998), leaving gaps in our ability to develop sound policy and practice across housing, leisure and land planning as well as health and social services.

Approaches to the conduct of research are also framed by a critical human ecology perspective. Clearly, environment must be taken into account. Further, value is placed on using a variety of methods, making increasing use of biographical and narrative approaches, considering older people as researchers in the entire research process and ensuring that we are critically reflective and self-reflexive in our work.

Being explicit about the values that underpin our work is an essential component of critical gerontology (Bernard and Phillips, 1998, 2000). For us, the critical gerontology we engage in is informed by commitments to: social justice;

countering stereotypes and combating myths and discrimination; citizenship and human rights; pluralist and positive views of ageing; making experience visible through the words of older people themselves; developing a critically reflective and self-reflexive approach to ageing – both our own and that of those around us; and an understanding of environmental context as being important. Such values will be articulated throughout this book.

Finally, the diversity of experience is to be valued. The diversity of ageing can only be understood by adopting multiple methods and perspectives on ageing. A critical perspective engages a variety of viewpoints on the experience of rural ageing, which links in with the multiple levels adopted by a human ecology perspective.

Structure and framework of the book

Chapters in this book reflect these values, assumptions and critical perspective. Our overall goal is to investigate the question: 'Are rural communities good places to grow old?'. We undertook this exploration because although rural areas often have a disproportionate number of older adults, little is known about the ways in which rural communities might be supportive to them. The contributors to this book consider this question from various standpoints, working in different rural settings, with adults at various points in their journeys towards old age. Scholars whose chapters make up this book are from Europe and North America. They come from a variety of disciplinary backgrounds: gerontology, family studies, sociology, human geography, demography, rural economy, human development, political science and material culture; but they share a passion for understanding experiences and processes of ageing in rural places.

Exploring the issue of whether rural communities are good places to *grow* old requires a lifecourse perspective. Understanding the pathways to old age is fundamental to a critical ecological approach. Throughout the book the lifecourse perspective is highlighted through the exploration of changing identities of older adults, their community engagement, and of shifts from support to care as people move into the last phase of their lives. The chapters are foregrounded in Chapter Two. Tamara Daly and Gordon Grant explore how rural places can create linked lives across the lifecourse. Following the critical human ecology framework of the book, they deconstruct notions of time, agency and location in time and space as they relate to rural ageing and disability.

Chapters Three and Four are about the connections of older adults to rural places and to people. In Chapter Three, Sherry Ann Chapman and Sheila Peace bring together the voices of older adults in England and in Western Canada to illustrate how identities of older adults are created and re-created in interaction with the landscapes that are integral to their lives. In contrast to the focus on the physicality of rural settings, in Chapter Four, Clare Wenger and Norah Keating consider ageing in the context of important people in the lives of adults as they reach very old age. Based on a unique longitudinal study of rural adults in Wales, they trace the changes in support networks among people who over 20 years become frail and in need of increasing levels of support.

There have been long discussions on both sides of the Atlantic of the challenges in providing services to older rural adults in widely dispersed communities. In Chapters Five and Six, authors consider strategies to support those who are the carers – both those who provide community-based services and those who are family members. In Chapter Five, Joanie Sims-Gould and Anne Martin-Matthews address the experiences of people providing home care in small communities. They articulate the issues confronted by people who live and work in small communities where the boundaries between personal and professional relationships are often blurred. Neena Chappell, Bonnie Schroeder and Michelle Gibbens in Chapter Six focus on family/friend caregivers to people in remote communities. They present lessons learned from intervention projects to provide respite to these caregivers who have little access to formal services because of their isolated location.

Communities that are good places to grow old in also provide opportunities for engagement and contributions and for social integration/connections. Rural communities may rely heavily on volunteers to help with creating and maintaining services, and to care for family and friends with chronic health problems. Chapter Seven places community engagement and contributions within lifecourse and rural–urban contexts. Janet Fast and Jenny de Jong Gierveld discuss the interplay of age and disability, and of urban and rural location, in determining social participation, and discuss the ways in which social participation might foster a sense of social integration. Chapter Eight builds on these findings, beginning with the assumption that, overall, there seems to be a good fit between rural communities' needs for participation and the resources of older adults to meet these needs. Julia Rozanova, Donna Dosman and Jenny de Jong Gierveld discuss the ways in which characteristics of rural communities may or may not foster social participation of older rural residents. In Chapter Nine, Bonnie Dobbs and Laurel Strain complement this work with data on the role of mobility in helping rural older people stay connected within their communities, discussing issues such as how ability to drive oneself versus being dependent on others can make a difference in community engagement.

The next two chapters are devoted to a critical analysis of community-level influences on inclusion and support of older adults. In Chapter Ten, Thomas Scharf and Bernadette Bartlam adopt the concept of social exclusion as a means to explore issues around disadvantage faced by older people in rural communities. The focus on social exclusion is important in casting light on the varied, and often hidden, nature of disadvantage experienced by rural older people in many Western societies. Jacquie Eales, Janice Keefe and Norah Keating in Chapter Eleven also address inclusion, but from the perspective of how community settings may create contexts that are 'age-friendly' and in which older adults are able to flourish.

In Chapter Twelve, Norah Keating provides an analysis of the main sets of findings from the book. These include increased knowledge about rural places and beliefs as they relate to the lives of older adults; about processes of ageing of rural adults; and about the interconnections between these places and processes and the contexts in which rural people grow older.

TWO

Crossing borders: lifecourse, rural ageing and disability

Tamara Daly and Gordon Grant

Introduction

This chapter introduces lifecourse perspectives that contribute to our understandings of ageing and disability in rural places; highlights what key assumptions about ageing, disability and rural places might fruitfully inform current thinking about the lifecourse; and raises questions for further research. As is evident from the preceding chapter, rural communities are defined in terms of locality and social representation, implying considerable heterogeneity in understanding of community types. When considering experiences of ageing and disability we therefore need to bear in mind how rural communities intersect in their diversity.

Four key lifecourse constructs identified by Giele and Elder (1998) are central to our analysis of future research areas investigating rural ageing and disability across the lifecourse. The first is *linked lives*, or social integration, the idea that all levels of social action (cultural, institutional, social, psychological, sociobiological) interact and influence each other, not only as parts of a whole but also as the result of contact with other people who share similar experiences. *Timing* covers the chronologically ordered events of an individual's life that simultaneously combine personal, group and historical markers. The next element, *human agency*, is embodied in the active pursuit of personal goals and the sense of self. Finally, Giele and Elder suggest that general and unique aspects of individual location affect personal experience and thus can be understood as being socially and individually patterned in ways that carry through time. They refer to this as *location in time and space*. We regard these four elements as useful framing devices to interrogate existing lifecourse analyses and to frame the research questions specific to ageing and disability in rural places that emerge from this book.

We start the chapter by briefly outlining the literature's progression from a lifecycle to a lifecourse framework. We then identify lifecourse theoretical advances related to ageing and disability in rural places. Drawing insights from multiple literatures, and using the lifecourse elements as our organising framework, we address how questions about ageing and disability in rural places challenge current lifecourse analytic boundaries by interrogating the fine balance among structure and agency; time, place and space; and identity intersectionality. Throughout this chapter, we introduce questions related to how heterogeneous rural contexts (for example, farming, resource extraction, retirement communities and so on) may affect each of the four lifecourse elements. We begin our exploration of challenging boundaries by raising questions about how rural places can create *linked lives* across the lifecourse. The remaining sections of the chapter deconstruct notions of time, agency and location in time and space as they relate to rural ageing and disability.

From the life stage to the lifecourse

In recent years there has been a shift away from construing human development and ageing as marked by a series of relatively predictable lifecycle stages. Terms like neonate, toddler, pre-schooler, pre-teen, adolescent, adult, third age and old-old still persist but in an increasingly postmodern world it can be argued that these categories have less and less meaning. Moreover, models that assume a connectedness between chronological age, human development and independence have been found wanting because they overlook the important idea that life is culturally embedded and socially contingent (Priestley, 2000).

The lifecourse framework assumes that individuals become more or less autonomous under conditions of changing cultural, social structural and historical settings, almost always entailing both continuities and discontinuities (Clausen, 1998). The paths taken involve twists and turns that result from complex interactions between a 'minded self' (human agency) and environments. This construction of the lifecourse is consistent with critical disability and critical human ecology thinking as articulated in Chapter One. It places an emphasis on understanding the physical, spatial, social and temporal contexts in which people live, as well as the ways in which individuals and their environments shape each other.

Linking rural lives

As Reeve (2002) suggests, disability and ageing are fluid concepts that are not fixed in time or place, and thus individuals' experiences vary. Following Riley and Foner (1968-72), ageing can be construed as a process that begins at birth, and is formed by experiences gained over the course of people's lives. They place emphasis on patterns that emerge over many years and involve multiple and often simultaneous life events (for example, parenting, and caregiving to a parent).

Disability can be construed as an ongoing process with landmarks, transition points and changing demands (Rolland, 1994). Disability may occur at any time across the lifecourse. It can be highly visible, as in the case of a mobility disability, or invisible, as in the case of Chronic Fatigue Syndrome. Disability also can come and go. For instance, the course of a disability may be progressive, constant or relapsing, so there may be difficulties with predicting what the future holds. Many individual accommodations, environmental adaptations and legal protections need to be in place to ensure the full participation of people with disabilities (Rioux and Daly, 2006).

The timing, course, accommodations, adaptations and protections associated with disabling conditions raise questions about whether all rural communities are good places to grow old. The important questions revolve around the extent to which living in rural places aids or diminishes people's capacity to fully participate. Are people isolated or do they develop different types of social networks? Are there ways in which rural spaces shape experiences of ageing and disability, thereby linking the lives of people living in rural places? What happens in families where children move far from home in order to work, while ageing parents remain in rural and sometimes remote places? How might this pattern of social connections compare with the situation in rural communities where in-migrants may have left behind established social networks?

Lifecourse and time

Conceptions of time are integral to an understanding of how the lifecourse is likely to be experienced. When considering temporality, Mills (2000) suggests the need to separate the natural from what is symbolically constructed within cultural and social systems. She demonstrates how *natural* or *cosmic time* remains relatively fixed across time and space, but temporal constructs such as historical, social, cultural and institutional calendars are perpetually in a 'state of becoming'. An example of natural or cosmic time is latitude and the related diurnal environmental patterns that shape daily rhythms and land use. Consider, for example, how the long, dark winters, frozen landscapes and isolated settlements shape the lifestyles, customs and health of the Inuit compared to the migratory patterns and subsistence economies of nomadic peoples in Tropical and Equatorial desert regions.

Another aspect of temporality is the internal clock of the individual, which can be divided into biological and psychological components. The *biological clock* is tied to the reasonably predictable circuit of the human body as it moves through its own physical timetable, with gender differences emerging in relation to health, co-morbidities and survival. *Psychological readiness* is also claimed to be connected to human development but it is now more readily accepted that self-identity formation reflects the interplay between historical, cultural and social contexts (Giddens, 1991).

Among more symbolically represented constructs of temporality, *historical time* is perhaps the most studied. Historical events are seen to shape a cohort, period or generation, and can encapsulate wide-ranging occurrences that have long-lasting effects – for example, war or economic depression. *Cultural and social time* also are important in this edited text. Cultural time represents the use and meaning of temporality manufactured in different cultures (Mills, 2000). Differentiation stems from how different cultures transform the social space and time to reflect unique ontological conceptions. Cultural time experiences are important in examining ethnic or religious communities – First Nations peoples, the Mennonites or the dominant cultural group in any society – or in coming to an understanding of practices that reflect diversity within multicultural societies. Social time, by contrast, refers to norms, values and rules about the time at which life events are expected to occur (Zerubavel, 1981). Social time conceptions have value in reaching an understanding of continuities and discontinuities in people's lives. Caregiver stress, for example, has been linked to the idea that families of children with disabilities can, over the years, find themselves caring 'out of time', for instance continuing to make decisions for adult children, although this aspect of their caregiving remains largely invisible (Todd and Shearn, 1996).

Finally, there are *institutional calendars* that can have a powerful influence on individual and collective human behaviour. There are the calendars of families as well as religious, educational, work and many civic institutions. These multiple calendars are often neglected and their importance underestimated for their effects and impacts on the way humans progress through the lifecourse. For example, for people with lifelong disabilities and those with adult-onset chronic illnesses, there is the prospect of negotiating transitions between health and social care services over the lifecourse. This can be particularly difficult when these services operate with different, sometimes even incompatible, schedules, values, philosophies and priorities. The achievement of seamless interorganisational relations in services remains a major structural impediment in meeting people's needs (Hudson et al, 1997). We suspect that, given the relative lack of formal service infrastructure in many rural communities (Tryssenaar and Tremblay, 2002), achieving conditions favouring seamlessness in service provision across the lifecourse for people living in these communities is difficult. This leads to important questions about how, and to what extent, informal networks and voluntary organisations serve to replace lack of formal supports. This issue is particularly important in rural areas that may be out of generational balance as a result of younger people moving away for work or the in-migration of older adults at retirement.

These clocks and calendars run parallel, together providing a powerful means of understanding how moments or periods in a person's or a family's life might be particularly important and require careful decisions or adaptations. They also have the potential to place a spotlight on both normative conflicts and asynchronous periods in the lifecourse when time clocks are running counter to one another. These are likely to be difficult periods for people. Both sets of timing issues are important in understanding the possibilities for adaptation and accommodation by adults with disabilities and older people in rural communities.

Lifecourse and agency

A lifecourse framework is well suited to examining how the individual level of analysis can accommodate how ageing and disability intersect in rural places. Heinz and Kruger (2001, p 41) suggest that 'the trend towards destandardisation and increasing individualisation of the lifecourse has been leading to more individual diversity in the timing of transitions, duration of institutional participation and sequencing of transitions'. They note that in postmodern societies a 'job for life' has long ceased to be the norm; changing fertility patterns and women's participation in the labour market have transformed notions of motherhood and associated assumptions about domestic responsibilities and contributions, while flexible retirement options have changed conceptions of how people construe time and use of time. Such destandardisation of the lifecourse may affect cohorts of younger people with disabilities more than others, largely because there may be more transitions to be faced in their lives than would have been the case for earlier cohorts. Construed in terms of the blurring of roles – for example between paid and voluntary work; work, employment preparation and unemployment; or receiving and providing care – destandardisation of the lifecourse may present opportunities for people with disabilities to assume a greater equality of experience with others. Equally, destandardisation may make it easier to predict what life holds.

Successful ageing theories, focused on individual agency, raise some pertinent questions for the rural context. Brandstadter and Grieve (1994) place an emphasis on the ability of older citizens to maintain personal continuity and meaning when confronted with different losses that accompany the ageing process. The assumption is that if goals and aspirations remain consistent with realistic options then successful ageing will be likely. In their theory of *selective optimisation with compensation*, Baltes and Carstensen (1996) adopt a similar position. Stobert et al (2005) note that those who age well are able to find the right balance among their level of activity, their life situation and their resources, an assumption congruent with that of 'person–environment fit' described in Chapter One. This finding is echoed in a social-psychological study of men aged 58-72. According to Crosnoe and Elder (2002), factors that helped define types of adjustments later in life included specific life issues and physical, psychological, interpersonal and social experiences gained over the course of the adult years.

In short, 'knowledge of the journey supplements knowledge about the destination in explaining patterns of adjustment in the later years' (Crosnoe and Elder, 2002, p 322). Interestingly, the well-rounded men were considered to be the most successful 'agers' because they excelled in multiple domains – not only at work or at home but also in the community, and not only in activity but also in their enjoyment of life.

In contrast, continuity theory (Atchley, 1999) suggests that over time individuals show a consistency in their patterns of thinking, living arrangements, social relationships and activity profiles, underscoring the importance of life history and biography to an understanding of experiences in later life. For instance, if personal continuity and meaning are important in understanding how people may age well, there is a need to be sensitive to factors that give rise to discontinuities across the lifecourse, and how these might be predicted, prevented or ameliorated. Living in rural areas, especially different types of rural areas, may make these possibilities more, or less, viable. However, Coleman (1997) warns that further development and testing of ageing theories is still necessary, and he reminds us that concentrating too much on how people age well risks overlooking the social construction and lived experience of impairments and chronic illnesses that can accompany the ageing process.

Theories of ageing well place high demands on individual agency. It should not be presumed that environmental supports necessarily will be in place. The case of single older people with fractured or unsupportive social networks (for example, Clare Wenger's careful research in rural Wales – see Chapter Four of this book) illustrates important variations in the structure and functioning of support networks for older people. A supportive, local community of interest is therefore likely to be indispensable to survival and quality of life for someone in a rural community who has mental capacity problems.

The kinds of questions raised about the notion of agency (identity, biography, personal capacity, personal values) suggest that if there is to be an accommodation of the structure–agency relationship, then service providers will have to work hard to achieve a sense of person-centredness (Williams and Grant, 1998; Mead and Bower, 2000) in the way they present themselves to people, particularly in reaching out to rural and remote communities.

Lifecourse and identity: location in rural 'space'

Lifecourse theory also informs our understanding of how cohort experiences of ageing and disability are influenced by structures such as the use of space, place and intersecting identities such as gender. We consider these next.

Space

One stream of lifecourse research looks at variation among and between different birth cohorts (Bury, 1995). This research places conceptual weight on the role of major social, cultural, political and economic events in shaping an identity among people born at the same time. Bury (1995) argues that the emphasis on the values and experiences of cohorts offsets what could become a disproportionate focus on individuals or on structures.

But lifecourse perspectives could approach the structure–agency debate differently. Setterson (2003) acknowledges that it is important to understand the environment as dynamic and changing. This is different from operationalising 'place' or 'environment' as a social structure. These constructs must receive more than backdrop analytical status, or be confined to descriptor status. Lifecourse analysis can draw its cues from critical disability studies where disability is viewed as largely dependent on the social, political and economic structures in which people's lives are embedded (Barton and Oliver, 1997; Rioux and Daly, 2006). If we accept that disability and ill-health are not simply biological states borne by individuals, but that environments and social structures construct disability and illness through a lack of appropriate accommodations, then it is important to ask in what ways rural environments shape and construct disability and illness as people age. For instance, buildings that are without ramps and are not wheelchair accessible produce a mobility disability that would otherwise not exist. Since long-term disability and chronic illness rates are higher in rural than urban areas (Rajnovich et al, 2005), we must look beyond individuals as the source of illness and disability, and consider how rural environments may socially construct disability and illness due to lack of appropriate accommodations or services. Such challenges will likely affect groups in different ways. Younger cohorts of people with disabilities residing in rural areas may have more technology and Internet familiarity than their older counterparts so their capacity for information retrieval and self-management may be much better.

Place

Insights from geography of health (Kearns and Gesler, 1998) show how place, which is an amalgam of identity and position, is an important construct for understanding shifting relationships between individuals, their families, the voluntary sector and the state (Eyles, 1985). Wenger (1990) points out that rural ageing involves unique relationships and structures that may persist across time and space.

If we relate these insights to the lifecourse framework, we might ask: in what ways do places and the way that public and private spaces are used structure life pathways, and impact on life meaning and experience? How do the characteristics and processes in spaces change over time? What are the interactions among individuals, families and place? Linked with the notion that social structures can create disability, how does the use of space in rural areas create illness and disabilities? For instance, what are the lifecourse implications when a workplace is also a home or when a farmer retires but continues to work the land? And what new accommodations are provided by new computing and telecommunication technologies that may allow older people in rural areas to access information and support in more timely ways?

Standardisation of public policies and services delivery may blur or even discount time, place and space commonalities and differences. Daly (2003) argues that rural providers of community support services in Ontario, Canada, indicate frustration with government funding rules focused on services and not recipients. In one example, ageing volunteers deliver services designed for older people's needs to people across the lifecourse who may be younger people with disabilities. The services do not necessarily acknowledge that illness and disability can be acquired at any time in the lifecourse, and that the types of services people need in their homes are place, space and person dependent. In other words, service needs must acknowledge place, space and personal specificities.

Intersectionality

A key criticism of the lifecourse as a conceptual framework is that it does not adequately theorise power relations. Bury (1995) addresses this issue by seeing one of the main uses of the lifecourse as an organising principle to look at the gendered dimensions of dependency, disability and inequality in later life. But he notes that the intersection of class and gender in later life has received relatively less attention. We know that care work is done primarily by women, most of whom are spouses. Women contribute more unpaid work (care for others, volunteer work, domestic work, childcare, self-care) than men across the lifespan, often with profound implications for care providers' health (Armstrong and Kits, 2001). For instance, more women than men report negative health consequences such as disrupted sleep, stress and physical ailments as a result of providing care work (Cranswick, 2003). It is not until retirement that men increase their participation in unpaid work although women continue to provide the majority of unpaid care work (Cranswick, 2003). Tasks are gendered across the lifecourse. Women contribute more care in the house including meal preparation and domestic work, and also personal care such as grooming, toileting, wound care, shopping and transportation. By contrast, men contribute more home maintenance such as work in the garden and repairs (Cranswick, 2003).

In a notable example, Hatch (2000) uses a lifecourse approach to show how processes of ageing are gendered. She notes that using it as an analytical framework allows researchers to consider the intersection or relations among multiple dimensions of identity (for example, 'race'/ethnicity, social class, disability, age and birth cohort, gender and sexual orientation). It also enables links to be made between sometimes simultaneous life trajectories such as work, childrearing and eldercare, each marked by different life events (for example, marriage, childbirth and getting a new job). Hatch's insights have potential to help reframe the lifecourse framework in ways that address questions of place and intersectionality such as how older adults may be prevented from undertaking transitions because, compared with other groups, they lack power. Questions such as the role of paid employment in people's ability to age well, or how socioeconomic and cultural issues in rural communities contribute to people's ability to age in place, are also questions of intersectionality. In rural and remote places where people negotiate their world on the basis of personal relationships, what does ageing look like?

People who are older and/or have disabilities do not necessarily view their lives through these lenses. Allen (1997), for example, reports that women with disabilities in her study related more to their gender than to their disability, and especially to their work roles, careers, family responsibilities and contributions to their communities. They described a network of resources, both environmental and from inner-self, as vital to coping with daily challenges. This finding is supported by findings from Peters (1996) who claims that people with disabilities want not only to make connections between their self-defined identities, but also to achieve what she terms 'border crossing', that is, to move seamlessly between the different roles and responsibilities that they enjoy throughout their lives. We need better evidence about the particular opportunities and challenges presented by border crossing for people with disabilities residing in rural areas whether, for example, accessing necessary health and social care supports, holding down a job, maintaining a family life and being part of the local community are realisable for individuals, and what factors enable this to happen.

Conclusion

In his seminal review of 20 years of lifecourse research and whether promises have been fulfilled, Mayer (2000) is far from convinced that the evidence yet meets expectations. He challenges us to think about whether or not there has been a rapprochement between structure and agency, between quantitative and qualitative research or between psychological and sociological approaches to lifecourse questions. He does point to exceptions like Elder (1974), who connected the adaptive capacities of people to differential resources and differential risk exposure, and also to Rutter (1996), who has demonstrated the multiplicity of bad and good emerging from adverse developmental conditions. Mayer (2000) is also critical of the failure of longitudinal studies to be used for purposes of evaluation of social policies. To this list we would add challenges associated with intersectionality (gender, 'race'/ethnicity, sexual orientation and ability) and place distinctions.

This chapter has considered the use of the lifecourse as a conceptual framework for critically understanding ageing and disability in rural contexts. It suggests that, in addition to time, lifecourse frameworks must confront notions about agency, social structures, place, space and intersectionality. However, it is suggested that the lifecourse provides a potentially powerful vehicle for understanding the interconnections between constructs of time that bear upon transitions and experiences in people's lives, the means for understanding and resolving asynchronous periods in people's lives and the potential for predicting and therefore controlling discontinuities. Yet we are still learning about how the particular demands associated with rural environments shape opportunities for adaptations for ageing well. How we understand those processes will be a key in deciding the most effective roles and designs for health and social care services in supporting older people in rural communities.

This book represents a step towards addressing these central questions about the lifecourse in that it brings together different but complementary disciplinary perspectives, different research traditions and different kinds of data – from longitudinal and cross-sectional studies, short-term and longer-term longitudinal studies, survey and narrative-based studies, theoretically driven and more applied studies and studies with different informant groups. The outcome, we hope, is a more enriched understanding of the challenges and opportunities for ageing well in rural communities in the 21st century.

THREE

Rurality and ageing well: 'a long time here'

Sherry Ann Chapman and Sheila Peace

Introduction

Throughout our lives the places in which we live reflect aspects of self. And, we reflect those places. In this chapter, we focus on rural place as a human ecological context and consider the impact for older women of choosing to age in such rural landscapes, contrasting the rolling countryside of England with the apparently harsher landscape of the Canadian West. Building on Rowles' (1983a, 1983b) concept of 'attachment to place' and working from a lifecourse perspective, we consider how the physicality of natural landscapes, in connection with social ideas about 'rural', may contribute to lifelong identities. We focus our critical lens on rural women who have been less visible than men in their relationships with the land, yet are core to Western beliefs in rural as a place of close kin and community (Little and Austin, 1996) and thus a good place to grow old. Referring to two qualitative studies in rural Canada and semi-rural England, we consider how women continue to find meaning as kin and community keepers in these places and how the choice to live there is part of their ageing well.

In Western society, due to increasing longevity, the concept of 'ageing well' is gaining renewed interest. One way to conceptualise ageing well is in terms of an ongoing process in which individuals make sense of their ageing amid later-life change (Chapman, 2005). Part of this process requires people to make decisions about how to live based on what is available in their communities. For example, what health and transport systems are available locally? What opportunities exist for socialising and for social support? Might individuals have to move to access key amenities, family and friends? As a result, do people perceive options (Peace et al, 2006) and/or feel constrained by the very places to which they have been long attached (Rowles, 1983b; Rowles and Watkins, 2003)? Such attachment is complex with potential changes across the lifecourse impacting personal affect, cognition and behaviour (Zingmark et al, 1995). Some older people may find themselves having to move from communities and places to which they are attached (Rowles, 1983b) and such change may influence how they make sense of who they are and of how they are ageing.

In this chapter, we explore the interdependence of older women with the rural landscapes in which they live. We reflect on whether these are good places in which to grow old and whether the physical and social character of place influences participants' sense of self in later life. We compare and contrast the lives of those living in two very distinct locations in the Western world. From the study of 'Environment and Identity in Later Life' based on in-depth ethnographic research with 54 older people living in South East England (Peace et al, 2006), we utilise case study data with five older women living in semi-rural Northamptonshire. From 'Caring Contexts of Rural Seniors', a three-year project in Canada, we draw on interviews with five older women living in the western prairie community of Oyen, Alberta. All of these women have chosen to stay in these places, in part because they have been "a long time here" (Greta, Canada). Some of the English women may have moved several times throughout the lifecourse but are now ageing in place, while the Canadian women have moved from family farms to a nearby town. Yet, even though their life histories may vary, their present experiences of rurality may reveal similarities as well as differences regarding how rural is a good place in which to grow old.

Understanding rural

Definitions of rural continue to change and to be redeveloped (Hughes, 1997) although, as indicated in Chapter One, conceptualisation in terms of population size, density and distance from urban centres is central. In urban Britain, a population of fewer than 10,000 may be seen as semi-rural, characterised by dispersed towns, villages and hamlets; remoteness is related to the number of households within a given area; and function is dependent on type of commercial activity. In Canada, communities with less than 10,000 people are considered rural, characterised by sparse populations across large distances and remote from urban centres (Rothwell et al, 2002).

The difference between the two is one of scale although similarities do exist. Rural areas tend to have proportionately more older adults than urban areas. In both countries there is evidence of young people migrating to urban and resource-rich centres for jobs, while older individuals age in place, and some retirees move to rural areas (Statistics Canada, 2001; Rothwell et al, 2002). In England, the work of Thomas Scharf and Bernadette Bartlam (see Chapter Ten) has begun to portray the advantages and disadvantages for older people of rural living with comments on reduced services, inadequate public transport, lack of affordable housing for younger family members and low income coupled with the changing population profile leading to loneliness and isolation that is fronted by stoical self-sufficiency. These factors are also seen in 21st-century Canada as economic trends influence the nature of family farming, the types of businesses that can 'survive' in small towns, the number of public services that can be supported and the very demographics of the farming communities (Heather et al, 2005). If social support for local older adults is diminishing as younger people move away for paid work, older adults' ability to age in place may be constrained.

Yet beyond such everyday realities, the term 'rural' is also used as a veil, conceptualised in social constructionist terms. In England, rural may define a retro-naturalness, 'an innocent idyll of bucolic tranquillity and communion with nature – a place to retreat from the ever quickening pace of urban living and to join in with "authentic", rustic community life' (Bell, 1997, p 94). In contrast, the Canadian West has a harsh ruggedness at the 'frontier' edges of Western society. In the past, this was 'no place for a woman' (Cavanaugh, 1997), with men best suited to this landscape. This social construction continues to inform a shared sense of Western identity evident, for example, in tourism information that celebrates cowboy culture (Alberta Tourism, 2007). Such locational symbolism can be linked in both places to the socialisation of women as kin and community keepers (Strong-Boag, 1988; Hughes, 1997), as the civilising element of the wild prairies or maintained through the local church or Women's Institute. In this way, the concepts of home and community that dominate conceptualisations of rural have been maintained and it is within this understanding that we situate the two locations.

Two contrasting locations

Oyen, Alberta

The Canadian data are drawn from the western prairie province of Alberta that has a growing provincial population (Statistics Canada, 2006). The town of Oyen is a farming community of fewer than 2,000 people located in the south-eastern part of the province (AlbertaFirst.com, 2007). It is a place with a relatively extreme landscape often characterised by the 'dust-bowl' drought of the 1930s; during that period, the relatively flat land was so dry that it cracked and blew away as sand, with the wind. Crop growth increased by the mid-20th century as moisture was relatively plentiful. However, as drought has returned in the 2000s (Schindler and Donahue, 2006), participants worry about kin who continue to farm and about their community. This is a powerful landscape where people share a sense that the place demands a heartiness to survive; for rural women in Alberta, this has meant an invisibility, as their kin and community-keeping work has been regarded as part of their 'helping' work to farmer husbands (Heather et al, 2005).

Northamptonshire villages, England

In contrast, Northamptonshire is a diverse county in England with a population of 646,700 in 2004 (Northamptonshire County Council, 2008) and where the patchwork of arable farmland and rolling hills is dispersed between Northampton town itself and a collection of smaller towns and surrounding rural villages. The participants contributing to this chapter come from Kettering Borough. At the time of the interviews, respondents lived in a range of settlements from the small town of Burton Latimer (7,100 in 2001) to the smaller village of Rushton (400 in 2001) to those living in more isolated farm dwellings on the outskirts of small villages. Research shows the changing nature of the commercial function within these communities, with people of employment age travelling beyond the village or small town for work but choosing to live within rural settings. For example, Burton Latimer had a population of 669 living in 143 houses by 1801. Census data from the middle of the 19th century show that farming was still the main employment for men in the village followed by shoemaking, stonemasonry, building and carpentry. Later developments saw the coming of the railway and commercial activity in terms of clothing and shoe factories, and a national cereal business. By 2001, the population had reached over 7,000.

While Oyen, Alberta, and Northamptonshire are very dissimilar, such dissimilarity is helpful for gaining insight into how natural places are inherent to older rural women's experiences of making sense of self and ageing.

Focusing on older women

There are many reasons for turning to older women. They may have held the role of matriarch or kin keeper within their community and yet, given their greater longevity, many will face end-of-life caring for, or living without, a partner (Bernard et al, 2000), often without local family support. While some may move, others will stay put. The physical and social dimensions of their rural places may influence their desire to remain. We consider their choices in terms of ageing well, despite the apparent harshness or lack of conveniences in their rurality. Do they identify with their rural landscapes? Are they attached to them? Do they consider their ageing in terms of their ability to continue to care for others, and for their homes? Our central questions for both groups are:

- How has the rural environment contributed, and how is it still contributing to participants' meaning-making about self and ageing?
- Are relationships with the natural environment (the land) a resource for growing old?

Who are they?

From a lifecourse perspective (Bengtson and Allen, 1993), all the interviewees were children or young adults in the 1920s and 1930s, experiencing the Great Depression. The Canadian participants come from farming communities, have white, European heritage and were either married or widowed at the time of the interviews in 2005. Some of them remember being on government food relief programmes during the Depression. During that time in particular, despite Western society's gendered roles, the source of many of their families' income came from women's 'egg money' and economising (Strong-Boag, 1988). On the prairies, participants survived their area's worst drought conditions of the century. From the mid-1950s through the early 1970s, they and their families also experienced the best conditions when the farming was good. At the time of the interviews, they were facing drought once again.

The English participants, in turn, survived the Second World War on their doorstep and the majority raised families amid post-war restrictions. Unlike the Canadian experience, the English population was highly urban by the 1930s. This meant greater industrialisation and fewer people living as farmers (Hicks and Allen, 1999). However, these participants have lived in semi-rural locations and small towns through their adult lives. Some had moved from one part of the country to another upon marriage, while others saw themselves as local. They are all white British and, with the exception of Ned and Neena (participants were given pseudonyms to preserve their anonymity), all were widowed at the time of the interviews in 1999-2000.

Ageing well in rural places

We turn now to the data to reflect on how experience of the natural landscape influences how these older women make sense of their ageing, and how these person–land relationships are a resource for their ageing well. First, we discuss how participants appear to relate to the nature of each place. Second, we consider how their socialisation as women to care for kin and community is tied to the nature of each place. Third, we reflect on how participants have lived interdependently with each place and how that interdependence is influencing their choice to remain in those places.

Among participants, the 'big sky' nature of Oyen, Alberta, has a harshness that is endured yet loved. Growing old in this environment is a process that occurs amid far-reaching horizons on some days and zero visibility on other days:

> 'During the Dirty Thirties, just prior to ... getting married, the fences that we had there, because the land blew so far here and the thistles grew, they were about the only thing, and they would catch on the fence and then that, that wind would just be constant, just be horrible, and eventually the dust and the dirt and the blowing sand took the, sometimes took the fences right off....' (Greta)

In the Oyen area, the climate demands a sense of self that can withstand the elements, and the recognition that moving to town might make growing old on the prairies easier:

> 'If it snows, someone's got to plough that snow so that you can get that car out, so that you can go plough [the farm's long driveway]. I would think it's easier living in town than on the farm.... But now that we're at our age, like I went to the fall supper with two [friends], one particularly, her husband passed away, and she's on the farm....

[I've told her,] "You can't stay there." ... "You're going to have to have help".' (Joan)

Yet, at the same time, this landscape and the lifestyle it demands are loved fiercely. It is part of participants' sense of self and how they remember who they are over time:

'We like it. We, we're used to it. We're used to being able to see two or three miles. We're used to the animals and the birds, and, the freedom. We're used to the freedom. And, our neighbours are close, usually. I know people. You know, if you know people, you're not worried about anyone breaking in. Or, whatever, you mostly know. The security.... That's what I mean by freedom. I just, ah, like, we were a mile and a half from our closest neighbour. [pause] That's a lot of freedom [laughing].' (Joan)

The Canadian participants demonstrate a lifelong adaptation to the demands and benefits of living in a harsh landscape. They live with this environment that is both dis-abling and enabling.

Similarly, in England, participants find security through the tranquillity of their location. Comments from Ned, a farmer, and his wife Neena, a person with mental health problems, suggest that a rural environment may support well-being in situations where living in a more densely populated situation may be felt as threatening and insecure:

'I would feel very lost if I couldn't see green fields out of one of my windows you see, from out there. I like to be in the countryside quickly ... I would find it very hard if I couldn't open that door and go into the garden. I would hate to live in a flat when all I have got to do is sit in a park. Very hard. I was thinking we ought to move, but I don't think it is on, I like it too much and ... it is the only place she has ever lived since we have been married, with this illness, that she has been happy.'

Even as the two places are strikingly physically different, both Canadian and British participants indicate a need to stay close to the land for reasons of grounding themselves in who they are.

The nature of these rural places influences how people relate to one another. The intimate scale of semi-rural English village life has meant informal community-keeping by women. Nerys reflects on the importance and influence of that socialisation. Her sense of self is rooted in her lifelong experience of her local community, which has supported her during times of personal loss (deaths of twins at birth and of her husband):

'I mean I can only speak from my own experience, but all I know is that ... when I had my twins I was amazed because I wasn't well known in the village ... however ... when I lost the twins it was staggering the stuff I got, bunches of flowers, a lady from the shop sent me a bottle of sherry. Things like that, and John [husband] would come in, I had been in bed for months, and he would say "oh who has done all the washing?" and I said "well this lady came and did it". You see ... you do find in a village, when my husband was very ill people left gifts on the door, things that they thought ... it is difficult to put into words, but ... you know that they will be there to give you a helping hand.'

In turn, Greta in Canada speaks of the demands made by the sheer scale and harshness of the Dust-Bowl Thirties for women to care for kin in particular ways:

'We had some *terrible* dust storms. There were some that came in so bad ... it was something black.... We don't have black dirt out here so it must have picked it up miles from here and it brought it along. And it got through everything, you know you couldn't put the food on the table without covering it with towels because of the sand. Anybody with babies had to wet-blanket the windows to, you know, so they wouldn't get, breathe in that sand.'

Also in the Oyen area, Emmy reminisces that her kin-keeping and socialising was organised in physical terms, around a farmyard shared by three generations:

'Our yard was the main yard, when the brothers [her sons] were starting to farm. The machinery and the cattle were there, and then you *always* had somebody in the yard. Someone coming in for coffee, the girls would come, my daughter-in-laws, come for coffee.... The kids come home on the bus; you wouldn't worry about them.... It was a good life.'

In both Canada and England, participants cared for kin and community according to the particular nature of their respective places and relative proximity to other people in those places.

The interdependence that participants have developed over time through living with and in these rural places is influencing their choices to stay there for the rest of their lives. Nancy, in England, shares her sense of self with respect to place: "Well, I suppose you can say I am a Burtoner folk now [laughs]. I think I have been here long enough now, yes".

In Canada, Margaret observed: "I think you'll always love the land once you've been a part of it". Margaret did not frame this as the land becoming part of her, which would be natural given Western society's understanding of landscape as a framed prospect hung in a living room (Bender, 1993). Rather, she spoke of being part of the land. Participants spoke of the land being their life. They knew and identified with their landscape based on their living with and in it:

> 'I still am a farmer. I still love the land. I love the prairie landscape. I always will. And, you know, I know the stuff that grows out there, and I love it. I don't see it very much, but I mean it's part of me and always will be … I grew here, up here and I've loved it all my life.' (Joan)

As they have aged, the Canadian women have migrated, but not too far; they are still in the same region. In contrast, the English women have aged in place. The question then becomes whether for these women the natural environment is a resource for ageing well and maintaining their identity for both groups of women.

There are positives as well as negatives. Location and distance from neighbouring places can be constraining and transportation is an essential element of being able to stay. Both communities have developed transport systems to enable older people to remain living in those places. Nerys in England states:

> '… we don't have any transport and I don't drive. I can't get out of the village unless I have a taxi. My husband [a parish councillor] started … he organised a minibus, that was voluntary … so that runs on a Monday, mainly to take the elderly to see their doctors … it goes … we get there about 9.50 and get to leave about 11am, you can do a bit of shopping if you want.…And then on Friday morning it leaves at … 9.30am from here and we leave Kettering at 5pm. So we get to do a little bit of shopping. I wait for my daughter and buy for two or three months, the big heavy stuff.'

Similarly, Joan in Canada says that:

> 'Every summer we've had a raffle to raise a little money, and it involved, you know, speaking to the government and getting grants and then finally getting a new, a new bus … which is, really, you know, it's such a blessing itself for seniors, because when you live in Oyen, if you don't drive a car, there's no taxi. You know, there's only 1,000 people … it's just not feasible financially to do that in here. So, ah, the Handibus, you can use it personally if, like if I was alone and I couldn't get out and I had a doctor's appointment, if, if you 'phone the day before, and it's all volunteer drivers.'

In addition, participants in both places have chosen to stay even though they live at a distance from additional social and health services more easily accessible in urban areas. In Oyen, participants spoke of a practical need to move from their farms to town as they aged. Yet they did not move to far-away large urban centres with extensive services. Rather, participants understand themselves in relation to the land and family and friends nearby in town and on local farms. Greta reflects on how:

> 'The kids have, have been after me … you know, to come and stay there [a larger town], you know, "If you retire…. We've got lots of facilities and things better…" But, you know, there's people here that you know [in Oyen] all, because you've lived your life – a long time here, I've lived – well, moved into [town] here in … [19]72.'

Greta also believes that Oyen is fortunate to have as many services as it does: "I think that we're very fortunate to *have* the things that we have right here in this town".

Nancy, who lives in Burton Latimer (BL) in England, reflects on the way an immediate engagement with the environment influences her views on moving to a more supportive accommodation as she ages:

> 'I did think about it, had a chance to have a flat in [sheltered housing scheme in BL] and that is … there's not a warden actually lives there but you've got the emergency bells, you know, if you wanted any help or anything but had the chance of one. I went, my friend lives in one, and the one she's got is on the opposite side of the building and you look all over the fields and it's lovely, you know it's really nice and bright and sunny. But this one I went to see that I got the chance of it was on the other side to the building just looking at the walls of the other flats and it was dark and dreary and as soon as I walked in I thought oh no that's not for me. I'd have to let me daughter have the dog 'cos, you know, you're not allowed animals there…. My home means everything, mine, I mean it's, well it's not mine, it's the council bungalow but, you know … I really am fond of my little bungalow and my dog.'

Despite these limitations, these women have weighed up the options and are choosing to remain in place because that is where their sense of self over time is located. Among the British participants, the respondents may not have been born and brought up in the places in which they now age and, with few exceptions, they have not been farmers. There may have been several moves across the lifecourse, but at this point staying put and remaining integrated within the community was more important than seeking a previous homeland. Nerys, who lives in Rushton, was born in a less affluent part of Wales and recently returned:

Nerys: 'I hadn't been back to Wales for 36 years, since I brought my father [here]. And after John [husband] died I had one

> school friend, and we have been friends ever since we have been school girls, and I had a great desire the following year after John died, I wanted to go back to Wales. She was telling me how the valley had changed, and was now this wonderful valley. It was a very beautiful place. So … I had a great desire to go back. And I went to stay with her, I hadn't seen her for 36 years, and … the first thing she said was [about the house I lived in]. I said "how much do they want for it?" and she said "£57,000 a lot of money" and I said "not to us". I couldn't believe it was going for £57,000.'

Interviewer: 'Did you go and look at it?'

Nerys: 'Oh yes, I went to have a look at it, and I said, "I could never live here".'

In Canada, when the Oyen women spoke in reference to their permanent moves to town, the migration to town did not mean a departure from their local region. They retained their sense of place and spoke of regularly visiting family who still lived on nearby farms. Even after this move, participants have continued to make meaning about the land, as they make sense of their selves and their ageing. Joan reflects on her relationship with the land:

> 'I guess it *has* been my life. *Completely*. It has been my life. It, it was my, income of my folks, poor though it was, and ours, and my children. It's, it's part of it. It's the land … I mean, these last few years with cattle problems and the *poor* price of wheat…. It's just terrible, and a high cost of machinery repairs, gas, that like, on the farm now everyone has two jobs. They're working to keep on the farm. But, but yes, the land has been my life, I guess.'

Worth noting is Joan's reference to family as an integral part of her growing old in that place.

Even as these two places are very different from each other, participants' experiences of ageing in the rural and semi-rural places are similar in their choices to remain in those places despite the constraints of requiring transportation assistance and, for some, living at a distance from an array of health and social services.

Conclusion

This chapter has provided an opportunity to enhance understanding about the concept of place in terms of ageing well, and how it is physically situated for these samples of older women. Their sense of identity as constructed with the land continues in later life, evident in their decisions to remain close to family, friends and that place. (In Chapter Eleven, Jacquie Eales et al also speak to the importance of family and friends, but note that older adults differ in the importance of having family members in close proximity.) This relationship was more extreme within the Canadian landscape and for women who had been directly engaged in farming. However, in both locations attachment to place was essential.

The environment contributes to participants' meaning-making about self and ageing in several ways. The natural elements, idyllic and/or wild, inform how participants have lived their lives. Their interdependence with family and community as kin-keepers is specific to these places. Their choices to stay within the immediate region have been informed, in part, by a desire to continue to experience the natural environment. Distances and the need for transportation are constraining to participants. (See Bonnie Dobbs and Laurel Strain, Chapter Nine, for a discussion of the importance of driving/mobility in the lives of older rural adults.) Yet, the natural place is so much of a resource for participants that, at times, distinguishing self from place is difficult.

In some of our examples we would argue that the relationship between gender, kin-keeping and community involvement enables older women to experience ageing well in different ways than older men. As younger women, the Canadians were all in helping work (for example, nursing, teaching, domestic work) yet that work was secondary to supporting husbands on the farm. Participants demonstrated that they continue to understand themselves in terms of a rural life in which their roles are to make their respective places more easily inhabitable for all.

To understand ageing well we need to understand the places in which participants are ageing and their relationships with those places. Our illustrations are from two very different locations. Yet these women know the land, and regard the physical landscape as one part of what makes a rural community a good place to grow old. This suggests the need to ensure that health and social services are maintained to support ageing in rural areas, if not in all local places, then at least in familiar regions. Considering and understanding the role that place plays enables the development of policies and programmes that support older rural women's quality of life, rather than force their departure from the places with which they know themselves.

Despite the social constructions of the rural idyll and rural wildness that require women to hold up the image of rural as a kin and community place, Canadian participants love the land, and their place in it, despite its harshness and their own invisibility there. English participants find comfort and maintain well-being within a semi-rural environment. Although communities are changing, our data show how community cohesiveness can support older people and how such collectivity may be more central to the lives of older women living alone. It is the changing nature of the populations and intergenerational exchange in rural life that may threaten this existence.

FOUR

The evolution of networks of rural older adults

G. Clare Wenger and Norah Keating

'They go with the family, their family … I think when you become frail or you're alone and you have no community resources – I don't mean physical resources; I mean family and very close friends – then, we find that that's why a lot of older seniors move.' (Service provider, retirement community)

'Yeah, I'm certainly being helped out…. Well, I don't think I could have stayed here without the boys helping me. They're not pushing me to move out and I would like to be able to stay here as long as I'm able. I'm not moving in with my family. That's not fair to them and they know that. It just depends on how much help you need I guess. I would hope it would be in a retirement home where I could look after myself and do well. But with, with help.' (84-year-old widow, farm community)

Introduction

People in one's life have been described as providing the 'meat and potatoes of social existence' (Garbarino, 1986, p 31). Supportive relationships are sources of love, intimacy and self-worth, providing tangible assistance and guidance (Lansford et al, 2005). Throughout life, good relationships are associated with better health, well-being and ability to cope with major life events. Lack of high-quality relationships is associated with negative physical and psychological consequences such as anxiety, depression, loneliness and poor health (Garung et al, 2003; Tyler, 2006).

Support to older adults is particularly important because of their place in the lifecourse. Normative experiences of death of parents, retirement, loss of a partner or close friends, or chronic illness make them vulnerable to the loss of social support (Garung et al, 2003). Across a number of countries including France, Germany and the US, researchers have found declines in social network size among older adults with such losses, although in other countries, including the

UK, Japan and Taiwan, networks are stable in late life (Wenger, 1989; Antonucci et al, 2001; Cornman et al, 2004).

Social network size is an important determinant of the potential for support. As illustrated in the quotes at the beginning of this chapter, older adults with no proximate social networks may have difficulty staying in their communities, while those with family members nearby may have good potential for assistance – an important issue for those faced with chronic health problems. Yet, social networks are not the same as support. Social networks are relatively objective – the 'warm bodies' in one's life. They are necessary but not sufficient for the active exchange of tasks and services. *Support* networks are functional subsets of social networks and comprise the members that provide emotional and tangible aid (Keating et al, 2003).

Which older adults are most likely to have rich networks of family and friends resources that they can call on? Network resources in old age are not universally available, but derive from the nature and type of relationships developed across the lifecourse (Aartsen et al, 2004). The term 'social convoys' describes those who progress through life together, and often is used to illustrate the evolution of individuals' personal networks (Ajrouch et al, 2005).

Families ebb and flow with births, marriages, divorce and deaths. Friendships may be lifelong or transitory depending on geographic mobility, opportunities through community, work or other connections, personal preferences and ability to reciprocate. People reach later life with differing sets of social resources they might call on for support. Older adults living in rural areas may have higher levels of social resources because of the contexts in which they live. Rural communities seem well positioned to provide strong support to older adults. A widely held belief is that they are particularly good places to grow old since people who live there are surrounded by family members, friends and relatives who will support or care for them as they age. Social convoys in rural areas are viewed as lifelong, stable and rich in diverse relationships.

This assumption is based in the idea that rural communities are problem-free environments where people share a set of values that include closeness to family, hard work and ties to the land (Shenk et al, 2002). In the UK, rurality has been described as having different problems from urban areas: separation from services and amenities (and thus safer because of its dislocation from urban areas), and less traffic but inadequate public transport, but greater visibility and higher community participation in voluntary groups (Wenger, 2001b; Atkin, 2003). Rural communities are seen as friendly and tight-knit, with shared values related to helpfulness and neighbourliness (Salamon, 2003). Proponents of this perspective speak of problems of 'rural dilution' as people engaged in primary production are thinned out by agricultural restructuring and in-migration at retirement leaving rural communities without a shared sense of identity (Smailes, 2002). Yet Sherry Ann Chapman and Sheila Peace (Chapter Three, this volume) argue that, regardless of connections to agriculture, the identities of longstanding residents of different communities in the UK and Canada are inexorably intertwined with the land.

Others such as Atkin (2003) and Thomas Scharf and Bernadette Bartlam (Chapter Ten) have begun to challenge this assumption of the idyllic rural life, arguing that rural areas are not always inclusive places for those who live there. They contend that rural people experience elements of social exclusion from the mainstream urban majority and that within rural communities certain groups are systematically excluded. This process of 'othering' may be applied to newcomers who look different or lead alternative lifestyles (Garland and Chakraborti, 2006). Horton (2005, p 425) is particularly scathing of the notion of the 'rural idyll', noting stark inequalities within British rural communities 'hidden behind a multifaceted jewel of scenery, outdated ideas of status and hierarchies, prejudice and even racism'. Similarly, Panelli and Welch (2005), speaking from a rural Australian perspective, talk about how a community ideal can be oppressive because it requires the homogenising of social identities and relations.

In this chapter we address the question of how the support networks of older rural adults evolve, change and adapt over time. We trace changes in social support of older adults across a period of 20 years, from their mid-sixties to the late-life frailty of those over age 85. Knowledge of supportive relationships of the very old is essential since with population ageing, the 85+ age group is increasing most quickly. Their networks are most likely to have had to adapt to increasing frailty and dependency, and this age group has people most likely to be in need of care. The question has been raised whether family/friend support networks in rural areas are able to provide and sustain high levels of care needed by older people with chronic health problems – in Chapter Six, Neena Chappell et al discuss the importance of respite for caregivers who otherwise have little support.

Understanding the support networks of older rural adults over time allows us to trace the evolution of networks in context. It helps us to begin to distinguish which older adults in rural communities are embedded in support networks that will evolve to provide care if needed. It helps us to deconstruct the idea of the universal supportiveness of rural communities.

Support networks of older adults

Researchers in different countries have begun to describe the convoys of social support surrounding older adults. Most of this research has been done in urban areas or among general populations of older adults and thus does not provide specific information about support in rural settings. However, it does illustrate diversity in the support of older adults. Typologies of support networks of older people have been developed in several countries, starting in the 1980s. Typologies developed in Australia (Mugford and Kendig, 1986), Canada (Stone and Rosenthal, 1996), Finland (Melkas and Jylhä, 1996), Israel (Litwin, 1995), the UK (Wenger, 1989) and the US (Fiori et al, 2006) demonstrate clear similarities.

All these published typologies include one type where older adults have small networks with few network ties. In Australia, Mugford and Kendig (1986) describe this type of network as attenuated, small with mainly tenuous ties. Stone and

Rosenthal (1996) found a similar type of network among older adults in Canada that is small, friendship-poor and socially isolated with little interaction outside the home except for minimal contact with children. In Israel, Litwin (2001) describes a restricted network of people who have little contact with their adult children, almost no contact with friends or neighbours and who are no longer likely to have a spouse. In the UK, this type of network has been characterised as very small with no local support. Researchers in the US have described two types of networks that are very restricted. These are non-family networks characterised by a low likelihood of being married; and non-friends networks characterised by a very low frequency of contact with friends (Fiori et al, 2006).

Family-based networks are another type of support network that occurs in all these typologies. These networks are small and focused on local immediate family. In the UK, this type of support network is associated with older and more dependent older people and other types of networks may become family focused with the passage of time and increased physical dependency if they include proximate kin (Wenger and Scott, 1996). Relatives are the main members of these networks and adult children are very important, although some older adults with family-based networks are actively involved with network members while others are not. These networks have few friends or neighbours. Such network types have been found in Australia (Mugford and Kendig, 1986), Finland (Melkas and Jylhä, 1996), the Netherlands (Aartsen et al, 2004), Israel (Litwin and Landau, 2000) and the UK (Wenger, 1989) and are more common at older ages.

The third type of network is friend based. Parallel to the family networks, these support networks are more or less intimate. For example, 'endowed networks' among Finnish older people include a large number of friends, at least one confidant, frequent meetings with non-kin and active exchange of practical help (Melkas and Jylhä, 1996). In contrast, 'friend-focused' networks in Israel have mainly friends; however, relationships are cordial but not intimate (Litwin and Landau, 2000). Friend-focused networks comprise between 12% and 28% of all networks.

The final network type is diverse, with a mix of kin and non-kin. Diverse networks are the largest of all network types and are typified by frequent contact with many kinds of people. Aarsten et al (2004) found that the majority of older people with diverse networks in the Netherlands have 14 or more network members, at least one friend and more than the average number of neighbours.

A striking finding from these cross-country analyses is the diversity in size and configuration of support networks. We do not know the extent to which diversity is a result of the variety of urban/rural settings or the cultural context of the various studies. The rural idyll might lead us to expect that support networks of rural older people would be predominantly large and diverse with older rural adults surrounded by networks of friends, neighbours and family members with whom they have ongoing contact. Yet pastoral communities mask exclusion of some rural residents, and smaller networks are also present in rural communities (Wenger, 1995).

Nor do we know whether different network types reflect people who are at different stages of the lifecourse since older adults in these studies range in age from their sixties to nineties. Thus we have snapshots of support networks but little insight into their evolution despite the fact that later life can span three decades or more, with its accompanying lifecourse events and entry and exit of support network members. If older adults develop chronic health problems in later life, support networks may be called on to evolve from sources of everyday interactions and exchanges to providing needed tasks and services to help older adults remain at home.

The evolution of support to care networks

In the remainder of this chapter, we draw on research on the evolution of support networks of older adults in a rural setting to illustrate how networks of older adults change over time in a rural setting. The Bangor Longitudinal Study of Ageing (Wenger, 1989) began with a representative sample of 534 rural people aged 65 and over living in small rural communities in North Wales. The study continued for 20 years with information on people's interpersonal networks gathered at regular intervals. At the end of the study there were 63 survivors, all over age 85. Half had moderate or high levels of impairment and needed high levels of support to remain living in the community. Such intense, ongoing support is often called care. Information on these very old frail survivors allows us to add to our understanding of support networks in rural communities and to expand our understanding of whether rural communities are good places to grow older, especially in the face of increasing frailty.

Rural Wales is an example of a particular type of rural setting with small towns (average population 3,000-4,000) at approximately 30-mile intervals, villages of a few hundred residents and dispersed upland sheep-rearing areas. The local economy is based on farming and is identified by the European Union as a 'less favoured agricultural area'. Despite short distances between settlements, there is only rudimentary public transport so car ownership is important. Older people continue to drive as long as they can and giving up driving is an important transition. In their research on driving and mobility, Bonnie Dobbs and Laurel Strain (Chapter Nine) found that those who no longer drive are at particular risk of losing contact with their social networks.

The main difference among communities is the proportion of in-migrants, particularly retirees, which is greater on the coast and near the border with England. The area is bilingual, with those who have always lived there being more likely to use Welsh while incomers are mainly English speakers. This difference exacerbates the difference between the indigenous Welsh and incomer English populations. The rural or seaside environment and scenery are important attractions to both indigenous and incomer populations as is the low crime rate, clean air and relaxed pace of life.

At the beginning of the study, 20% of participants were childless. They had married late as a result of experiences as young adults with world wars and economic depression. Many with children had none living nearby, because of their retirement migration or because their children had left their communities to find work. In comparison with more urban communities in the UK, more of these older adults attended religious services and meetings of voluntary organisations, indicating greater community integration.

The variety of experiences of these older adults was reflected in the diversity of their support networks at the beginning of the Bangor study (Table 4.1). Even as relatively young older people, they already differed considerably. The composition of their networks reflected their own lifecourse events and decisions such as whether they moved to find work or had migrated to North Wales and away from longstanding networks of family and friends on retirement. Networks also reflected family lifecourse changes that were not always under their control, such as whether they had already been widowed or their children had migrated out to find work. They also differed on factors such as community connections and personal traits that made them more or less likely to be actively engaged with others.

Table 4.1: Distribution of care network types of frail older adults and their support networks in 1979 and 1999 (%)

Network type	1979 (survivors) aged 65+ (N=63)	1999 (survivors) aged 85+ (N=63)
Family dependent	8	24
Locally integrated	41	21
Wider community focused	22	10
Local self-contained	21	13
Private restricted	6	29
Missing/inconclusive	2	5
Total	100	100

Note: Columns may not add to 100 due to rounding up.

Two groups of older adults had networks with nearby family members at the core. Those with family-dependent networks had relatively small groups of close and extended kin who provided emotional and practical assistance when needed and included the older person in ongoing family activities. They liked being able to count on their families for inclusion in activities although they did not turn to them for a great deal of ongoing support. People with this type of network said things like: "I'm very lucky to have my family around me. They'll take care of me if necessary".

Those with locally integrated support networks had the added advantage of groups of friends and neighbours that fostered links to the community as well as local kin. Their networks were rich in both kin and friends. People with this type of network felt well supported and were able to reciprocate the assistance they received. These people were likely to say: "We all know one another round here and look after each other. There's always someone popping in to see how I am". This type of network approximates most closely the stereotype of rural life and was the predominant network type. As Table 4.1 shows, 41% of older people had this type of network at the start of the study, a much higher proportion than those with the narrower family-only network (8%).

In contrast to those with networks including local family, a third group (22%) had no local kin and had networks mainly of friends and community contacts and regular contact with relatives living at a distance. However, people with these wider community-focused networks were well integrated into their communities through friends and local voluntary organisations, despite having few kin nearby except for spouses. While they missed having family members in the same village, they felt that they could count on their friends for everyday support: "Although all my family live away, I'm lucky to have good friends nearby and they'd help me if I needed anything". The majority of participants had one of these three types of support networks, each of which helped keep older people connected to others in their communities. For them, social settings did seem to reflect a rural community ideal.

In contrast, two other groups of older adults had more limited support networks, little or no involvement in their communities and no close kin living nearby despite having lived in the area for long periods of time. Many with locally self-contained networks were childless. They tended to be somewhat solitary, enjoying their own company. Although they were reluctant to ask for assistance, they believed that they could rely on neighbours if necessary: "I'm quite independent and keep myself to myself. But I know that the neighbours are there and would probably help me if I needed anything".

Those with private restricted networks were more socially isolated with even fewer links to others outside their households, although more were married. They tended to have lifelong patterns of social isolation. A typical comment was: "I don't have much to do with the people round here but then perhaps I've always been too independent (or too much of a loner)".

Adults with both these types of networks received little informal assistance unless they had a spouse. Their relative isolation in small rural settings belies the stereotype of the rural idyll as a pastoral setting in which strong community networks foster inclusion of those who live there. At the beginning of the study, 27% of participants had one of these two network types.

In these five different types of support networks one gets a sense of the diversity among older adults and the differential likelihood of receiving care later in life should they require it. Among those with close kin as core network members (in family-dependent and locally integrated networks), care may be available since family members generally have high normative expectations to provide support (Keating et al, 1999). Those with wider community-focused networks seemed to epitomise the kinds of support we expect from rural communities. They were well integrated into their communities through friendship networks, had large networks and often were active volunteers and community members. Many were retirement migrants, but if they were longstanding residents, the social capital they have developed over years of community engagement may serve them well. In contrast, the two sets of older adults with small, household-focused networks received little day-to-day support, had no apparent network with which they exchanged everyday tasks and services and had low care potential.

Twenty years later: convoys or isolation?

Over 20 years the distribution of the support networks of these survivors changed substantially (Table 4.1) as survivors reached very old age. At that point, participants had an average age of 93, with the youngest being 85. There were two main trends. The first was that networks that had had proximate relatives as core members shifted towards even more of a family focus. Family-dependent networks increased threefold. The proportion of locally integrated networks was reduced by half, as many shifted towards family-dependent networks. Most networks that evolved from these two groups were based on a wife, husband, co-resident adult child(ren) or occasionally daughters, grand-daughters or sisters living nearby. In most cases one or two key caregivers provided all necessary care to enable the person to remain in the community.

For most of these survivors with family-dependent and locally integrated networks, their networks responded to their increased needs while helping them to remain at home. Where networks were very small, homecare was used to supplement family resources. For the remainder, catastrophic events affected the older adults or their potential carers, thus exceeding families' ability to provide care at home. For example, a stroke experienced by one older resident resulted in paralysis and incontinence that made care at home unfeasible. In another situation, a daughter who might have been a main caregiver was widowed, requiring her to delay retirement and put her energies into supporting herself. In both situations, the older person was admitted to residential care before a care network developed in the community, although pre-existing networks continued to provide emotional and material support.

The second main trend was that compared to 20 years previously, only half as many very old adults had had friendship-centred (wider community-focused) networks. Among those with the most limited support networks, there was a shift from local self-contained to the more solitary private restricted network type. The latter increased from 6% of networks to 29% 20 years later, a shift towards very small, household-focused networks with no proximate kin unless they had a spouse. The shift here was driven by deteriorating health, increasing frailty and the death of spouses or other potential carers. Networks also became private restricted when the older person was severely mentally impaired or in the final stages of terminal illness.

In contrast to those with family-focused networks, only 20% of older adults with these limited networks received care from network members. The majority were retirement migrants. More than half had no children of their own and the remainder had children living more than 50 miles away. Many were able to survive in the community with the support of formal domiciliary services, such as household help, homecarers, meals on wheels and/or community nursing services.

Conclusion

Clearly, rural communities are not universally supportive to those who in advanced old age are increasingly frail. The example in this chapter from rural Wales showed that the network resources of older adults were influenced by the rural contexts in which they lived, the history of their convoys of support and their increasing frailty.

At the beginning of the study, surviving participants were in their sixties and had a variety of support networks. Their network types were similar to those found in a number of other countries. However, higher proportions of these rural residents had networks that included a variety of family, friends and other community members, suggesting that for them, rural contexts are rich in their social relationships. Nonetheless, there were also seeds of isolation in those who had small networks or who had potential networks but did not actually call on them. These less integrated adults may not have been full participants in social relations because of 'othering', which kept them outside of active engagement in their communities. Some of them had always been loners and others had developed independent lifestyles of self-sufficiency. Similar to the 'stoic' older people described in Chapter Eleven (Jacquie Eales et al), they had not sought nor maintained strong linkages to others in their communities.

Other research in the UK has shown that personal conditions such as poverty or community changes including lost services such as post offices and shops are barriers to engagement in community activities. In speaking of disadvantage in UK rural communities, Thomas Scharf and Bernadette Bartlam (Chapter Ten) report that for older rural people who are disadvantaged by lack of income and chronic health problems, ageing in place is a cause for concern. For participants in their study of rural communities, the idea of 'being part of a vibrant community characterised by close bonds between local family, friends and neighbours did not appear to hold true for all' (Scharf and Bartlam, 2006, p 3).

As support networks of older adults in rural Wales evolved over 20 years, they became much less diverse. The main shift was towards one type that provided high levels of care, mostly from close kin, and another in which care networks were tentative and unable to sustain the levels of support needed by these very old, frail people.

What happened to their social convoys over 20 years as people aged and developed chronic health problems? When faced with declining health, some rural older adults without nearby relatives left the community because they could not manage even with the formal services that were available. The quote at the beginning of the chapter illustrates the difficulties faced by those without proximate kin.

Yet friends and neighbours were less involved in care than we might have expected given their presence in a number of the support network types at the beginning of the study. In fact, non-kin had only tangential roles in providing care. This finding is contrary to our expectations that rural communities are inclusive of older adults who are broadly connected to other community members. It also is in contrast to research in Canada on care networks of frail older people, which shows that more than half of their care networks include at least some friends and neighbours (Yoshino, 2006). Those with longstanding mental illness are especially vulnerable to isolation from friends and neighbours. In the Netherlands, Aartsen et al (2004) found that cognitive decline led to lost relationships with friends and neighbours that were not replaced by kin.

The focus of care by close kin in the North Wales communities results in part from the household configurations of the very old survivors. Parents sometimes shared households with adult children because the children had not left home, particularly in farming families. Such arrangements may be undertaken as an exchange of access to the family business for provision of care to parents (Lashewicz et al, 2007). Alternatively, a joint household may be re-established for the benefit of the younger generation in need of housing (Wenger et al, 2002). In such situations, family care is reciprocal and may not reflect lack of interest of community members.

One of the side-effects of longevity for the oldest old is the loss of potential carers through death or disability. Widowhood was common as were the deaths of children and/or children-in-law. While not all deaths of the next generation directly affected the care situation of older persons, some did, and all reduced the pool of potential carers as well as potential sources of support or respite for adult children who became carers for their parent/s. Other lifecourse issues of next-generation kin also influenced their availability as caregivers. Many were themselves nearing retirement and continued full-time employment was an important element of their own pension rights. Several were unable to provide care or to maintain care at increasing levels of dependency because they needed to work full time.

For very old adults, rural communities can be either highly caring or socially isolating. The potential for caring is evident much earlier in the composition of their everyday networks of support. Convoys of support are fluid but have predictable trajectories towards very late life. While a variety of people may be the meat and potatoes of social existence, families are the stuff of difficult times.

FIVE

Distance, privacy and independence: rural homecare

Joanie Sims-Gould and Anne Martin-Matthews

'Oh, the other thing that's fabulous here, which I didn't even mention, I think, is this homecare thing. Has anybody talked to you about that? They have this through the [agency name], and you can stay in your own home until you're practically at death's door because they'll come and get you up in the morning. They get your breakfast. Somebody comes to get your lunch. Somebody comes and gets your supper. Somebody comes to put you to bed. It's wonderful. Of course, you know them all, you know, because they were friends and neighbours. They're your friends' kids or something, you know, and it's a wonderful thing.' (Older woman in rural Canada, receiving home support)

Introduction

For many older people, ageing in place is enabled by a frequently complex system of support comprised of relatives, paid or formal caregivers, neighbours and friends (Sims-Gould and Martin-Matthews, 2007). The receipt of adequate and appropriate homecare[1] is one component of the formal service sector that contributes to the likelihood of older rural residents remaining in their homes and communities.

Homecare is an expanding sector of healthcare delivery in many countries around the world (Hall and Coyte, 2001; McClimont and Grove, 2004; Broese van Groenou et al, 2006). Overall population ageing, combined with a strong desire to 'age in place', creates an increased likelihood that many older people will use homecare. The increased likelihood for use of homecare also exists within many rural and remote areas around the world, particularly in the absence of local hospitals or other acute/post-acute care options. This chapter examines the experiences of home support workers and older clients in the delivery and receipt of home support services in rural Canada.

The receipt of appropriate home support services enables many older people to remain in their homes and communities as they grow older. In rural areas, home support services are particularly important in that they can often prevent or delay the relocation of an older person to an urban centre where hospitals, acute and post-acute care are more readily available. While there is a growing body of knowledge on homecare, few studies have examined home support in the rural context (Williams and Cutchin, 2002; Canadian Homecare Association, 2006). These studies have focused largely on rural health service delivery and physician recruitment and retention, and have identified such issues as geography and location (Parr et al, 2004), lack of service and/or limited availability of services (Virnig et al, 2004; Merwin et al, 2006) and recruitment and retention of healthcare workers (Minore and Boone, 2002; Harding et al, 2006) as central concerns in rural communities. While these studies have focused on the physical geography and the economics of homecare delivery in rural places, this chapter focuses on the experience of providing and receiving community-based health services in the context of rural environments.

Our analyses draw on data from four Canadian studies that include the perspectives of both home support workers and older adults receiving homecare. Communities cannot be supportive unless those who work in them like what they do and believe that they can do a good job (Gardiner et al, 2006; Eley et al, 2007). Similarly, rural communities cannot be supportive unless those who receive services feel that their service and support needs are adequately met. To better understand the experience of providing and receiving home support services in rural areas, our research is framed by human ecology and examines issues of distance, privacy and independence as important elements of the rural homecare experience.

Distance, privacy and independence: an ecological perspective

When a human ecological framework, focused on the contexts in which people live, informs the study of homecare and home support, attention is placed on the dimensions of environment, relationships and person, from the perspectives of both providers and receivers of homecare. Home support is embedded within larger socioeconomic, cultural and political contexts. Older clients, formal caregivers and family caregivers negotiate the boundaries between private home life and public healthcare work, which, in turn, is mediated by the structures of social, spatial and temporal environments of the private residential setting and the organisational environment of the homecare agency, as well as the public healthcare system (Mahmood and Martin-Matthews, 2008). Issues of territory and boundary, control and cooperation, and the symbolic significance of home are central to the experience of home as the site of care (Martin-Matthews, 2007); however, analyses of the verbatim accounts of rural homecare workers and older clients suggest additional issues that characterise the rural homecare experience – for both receivers and deliverers of service.

Analyses of our data on rural home support identify several themes that reflect the social, spatial, temporal and organisational domains of home support. Transportation and distance are key environmental concerns reflecting the spatial, temporal and organisational aspects of rural home support. Privacy – always an issue when public services are delivered in private settings – is a particular concern in the social dynamics of home support providers and receivers in rural areas. Issues of independence and autonomy reflect the agency of the person at the centre of the delivery of home support service.

Transportation and distance

'Our community … one of their big concerns about homecare is that it's so expensive to deliver homecare. It's not so much the huge distances, but it takes a long time to get somewhere. So you may be riding an hour, an hour and a half, or two hours to get to a client and then the same distance back.' (Home support worker)

'Travel is a real problem. Distances are really great between clients and in the winter it is terrible. Sometimes I feel the [agency name] office is too distant to have our interests at heart.' (Home support worker)

As indicated in the above quotes, travel and scheduling are areas of concern for workers, clients and agencies. These issues have particular salience in the rural homecare context. Home support workers and older clients emphasise issues of time, safety concerns, inclement weather and poor road conditions, petrol (gasoline) prices and agency interests as influencing delivery and receipt of rural home support services. Few clients and workers commented solely on transportation and distance, but rather focused on the broader context of challenges to accessibility and delivery of services because of additional, and often compounding, issues.

Safety and inclement weather are challenges for many rural home support workers. Not only do they have to travel long distances between clients, but inclement weather such as blowing snow, freezing rain, hail or the presence of wildlife make hazardous road conditions more precarious. Travelling in the winter can create additional safety concerns for home support workers who work in a rural environment.

'Distance would be a challenge sometimes, especially in winter, providing that caring to people. We have people, well, they're probably 27 miles from town. Well, if it's miserable weather and whatever, it's always a challenge. It's a challenge to us, too, because it's a safety issue, travelling on the bad roads, storms or whatever. Even getting to somebody's place if it's storming, you never know. That's a hindrance.' (Home support worker)

Costs related to petrol prices and wear on vehicles from driving long distances on unpaved roads again are additional challenges for home support workers working in rural environments.

'It's farther to drive, it's mostly gravel roads, I'm not charging mileage, and I'm thinking if the gas prices go up, I'm going to have to figure out a way to work out some, because I'm going over 40 kilometres to some.' (Home support worker)

'But it is a challenge for me charging the same rate as the ones in town, because I just burn so much more gas, everything, going everywhere so. And I have to get up a lot earlier, like if I'm going to be at somebody's place at 8 I'm up at before 6, because it takes me three quarters of an hour to drive there. So, um, that's another, that's another hardship for me to provide that service.' (Home support worker)

Transportation and distance are also influenced by living conditions and quality of housing in some rural areas. One home support worker noted that while transportation is a major issue, the unavailability of electricity and/or running water in clients' homes provides unique challenges to the delivery of appropriate and needed services.

'I think for some of these people transportation is a major, major, major issue … we're also finding places where they still may not have chosen to [have] electricity or running water. Those are particular challenges. They've lived with it and can make their bread and that kind of thing, but it really introduces a special element when it comes to end-of-life care in a setting like that.' (Home support worker)

These factors – extended travel time, inclement weather, safety concerns and petrol prices – all contribute to how distance and transportation are experienced by rural home support workers.

Privacy

'It's hard because you might keep it confidential or the staff here might, but I've been in the post office and heard stuff that totally, totally might be about one of our clients. It's not us saying it, but people are talking about it because they know. That's a small town; everybody knows everybody's business. I've been in the post office and the lady has proceeded to show me that she's got a boil on her boob. That's not [over] the line; it's happened to a few of us. So, you know, just wait, I'll be to your house to visit you. Like, it's hard. I mean, you might not be saying anything, but there are so many other people that know everything.' (Home support worker)

Issues of privacy and territory are concerns expressed by home support workers, their older clients and family members. In rural areas, home support workers and older adults have additional and unique confidentiality and privacy concerns, particularly so in very small rural communities where 'everyone knows everyone'. Lack of privacy and anonymity contribute to an older person's and their family's resistance to using support services (Morgan et al, 2002). This causes anxiety on the part of older clients who worry that 'their business' may become gossip but is also a concern for home support workers who want to maintain healthy boundaries between work and home life. The tension comes from the blurring of professional and personal boundaries. Home support workers and clients in rural communities work and live within the same local spaces where chance meetings are likely and can be frequent, thereby creating a dynamic where individuals feel exposed, even vulnerable. Workers may be approached in public spaces with questions better suited to the confines of the professional relationship. In rural areas, work life, home life and healthcare may be difficult to compartmentalise, creating particular challenges for providers and receivers of homecare.

> 'I draw the line. My first two years was very difficult because I fell in love with everybody I worked for, and when I would come home at night they would call. "Well, I need milk and I don't have any." And I would have to say, "That's not my job." That's a very difficult part, but you have to draw the line. If not, you'd have a nervous breakdown. And it's regulations, plain and simple, so you do your job, you do your job well, but when you come home, you hang your coat up. That's your job.' (Home support worker)

Despite these challenges, home support workers and older clients also acknowledge the benefits of living in a rural environment and its positive influence on their worker–client relationships. Home support workers may have a more intimate knowledge of the client's community environment. A worker's local knowledge of the resources and opportunities in the community may ultimately benefit their clients and, for the client, may facilitate and strengthens their relationship. An older client says:

> 'The homecare [worker], she stays for two hours. She came here and said, you know, there's fish for sale over in, the IGA for, cheaper than you know, than they've been. And she had got some and said they were good, and she said I'll slip over and get some if you want them. So I gave her some money, and away she went.... And that's probably beyond what her job is, but, that's just the kind of people.'

For clients too, rural environments and, especially, close-knit rural communities, may enhance the homecare experience, with clients and workers having a more detailed and intimate understanding of one another's social networks.

'I think that in a smaller town you have better homemakers because you get to know their family, etc. It's much more personal, quality care.' (Older client)

Independence and autonomy

'I think you sometimes find, the mentality in small rural community of "I can look after myself, I don't need help, I'll do without". That sort of thing. "I can take care of myself."' (Home support worker)

'Not even Carolyn, who is my mother-in-law. She doesn't want her to clean the house. Although she's been in the house and visited them, she doesn't want her [home support worker] there to clean. She doesn't want nobody there cleaning, which is interesting because I think that if I was that old and had been doing it all my life, I'd be like: yeah, somebody's doing it for me finally. You know? I think that's their generation's mentality, though. Everything was done by them, and that's all.' (Family member)

In the quotes above, both home support workers and older clients and family members see a set of beliefs about independence, hardiness, the ability to work, self-reliance and practicality, also noted by researchers (Anderson et al, 2000). These qualities have been associated with delayed help-seeking (Morgan et al, 2002), with cultural and social values in rural communities having an effect on when individuals access homecare services. In many places, rural residents receive less homecare assistance than their urban counterparts (Forbes and Janzen, 2004; Virnig et al, 2004). A home support manager said:

'There's a cultural challenge in trying to bridge that gap between their perceptions of how to work with us and with any service agency because they're grand, their parents have, by tradition, been extremely self-sufficient, reliant on themselves and their family, maybe their closest neighbour. But they're not accustomed to using social service agencies.'

Such refusals are not necessarily a uniquely rural attribute, and have been identified more broadly within the home support research on older clients (see Martin-Matthews, 2007). However, independence and self-reliance are articulated in a number of the verbatim responses from rural residents. Older clients, family members and home support workers all characterise self-reliance as a key issue accounting for many of the refusals of services or lack of interest in receiving them.

While independence and autonomy may be cultural values that delay or impede the uptake of home support services, there are two additional explanations. First, relying on oneself is a more cost-effective alternative; refusal of service may be an economic consideration above and beyond anything else. A home support manager acknowledges this difficulty:

'The ones out there [in the] country are much more independent. And I think it's just that much harder for them to go, you know what, I think I'm going to have to pay somebody to help me. I know that the ones that I'm going to aren't living on a really tight budget. So I think it's more the idea of oh my gosh we gotta to pay somebody to help me do this, you know, that's a big step for a lot of them. To ask for help, I think.'

Second, the types of services available may not meet the needs of older clients. For example, in the qualitative data we reviewed, older clients and family members commented on a need for assistance with home yard maintenance, snow removal, transportation and shopping for groceries. Refusal of home support services in these instances is less likely to be related to a value of independence and autonomy and more a function of a difference between needs of the older client and the types of services offered as a component of home support. For example, neighbours said:

'That's where I'm going today. To bring up one of the ladies that lives up here. Now she … had a hair appointment. And she couldn't get a hold of a taxi; there's only one taxi here in [name of town]. And uh, she couldn't get anybody, so I took her down. So that's why I have to go to pick her up now at 4:00. But I don't mind doing that. Not in, not in the summertime. But in the winter … boy, it's different. You know, a different thing. Now we have another lady over here. She's, um, she must be about 87 or 88, I guess, and she calls me quite a bit, and I take her down for groceries and that sort of thing. But I don't mind doing it. I'm going down usually anyway. But as I said, once when it gets icy, well, I don't know what they're going to do.'

'My next door neighbour.… We make sure our sidewalk's shovelled; we make sure she is ok. There's another girl that comes in once every two weeks that cleans her house and does a little bit of banking. But who picks up her mail and the little things? My daughter goes to her house and does her hair and she said, I can't do that for everybody's mum, in town because I need my business in my shop but she does it for Vi next door because she knows that I'm looking after her.'

Conclusion

> '... there's a lady right now in [community name] who's living in her trailer and she's managed to pay it off and she's got it beautiful, the way she wants to have it, and we're encouraging her to move to the Lodge [in a city] because of her health concerns. That makes you stand up and say, are we impacting these people moving to the Lodge when in fact could community ... maintain [her] in her home, where she's very happy.'

For most older people, a good place to grow old is one that enables them to age in place, maintaining their own home and living independently for as long as is possible. The ability to age in place successfully is influenced by the availability of, and access to, an appropriate mix of formal (paid) and family, friend and neighbour supportive health and social services. In rural environments where the range of supportive paid services may be more limited, accessing appropriate and adequate formal services can be difficult. There are also challenges in delivering and receiving these services. For example, Jacquie Eales et al (Chapter Eleven) show that older adults in rural areas differ considerably in seeking and gaining access to formal services. In remote communities that lack a formal service infrastructure, successful interventions have focused on supporting family members and friends who have most of the caregiving responsibility (Neena Chappell et al, Chapter Six).

As shown in this chapter, living and working in a rural community can pose specific challenges to the delivery and receipt of homecare services, including transportation, distance, weather and lack of available or appropriate services. The nature and dynamics of relationships in home support are also distinctive in rural communities. In particular, in very small places, home support workers do not have the same anonymity that workers in larger places experience. Our findings show that it is not unusual for older rural residents to have a home support worker who is also a friend's child, a neighbour or even a relative. The duality in relationships and the often small number of interaction places (for example, only one postal outlet) create opportunities for older adults and workers to chance meet outside of the working relationship. These chance meetings can benefit client–worker relationships, but they can challenge the maintenance of boundaries between workers' home and work lives, and clients' personal lives and 'public' health concerns.

Independence and autonomy were also reflected in our findings. Rural identity intertwined with family history, land use/ownership and culture are strong ties for older adults (Sherry Ann Chapman and Sheila Peace, Chapter Three) that translate into a strong sense of self-reliance and an equally strong desire to age in place. However, both rural identity and financial constraints may account for failure to access appropriate services to meet rural residents' needs. In addition, as Williams and Cutchin (2002, p 110) argue in the Canadian context, 'rural areas can be viewed as experiencing a "double burden" where problems of poor professional availability and accessibility are made worse by government policy that does not recognize the circumstances and needs of non-urban places'. Similarly, Sherwood and Lewis (2000, p 337) suggest that with the 'rationalization and centralization' of services in England, services have been developed with an urban-centric focus. Political decision making has an important role in determining the delivery of care in rural communities and whether the challenges of delivery are realised (Williams, 1999; Sherwood and Lewis, 2000; Williams and Cutchin, 2002). Policies that guide home support programmes must attend to rural environmental circumstances. As an example, with transportation and weather as acknowledged concerns in rural communities, home support workers employed in these areas need extra paid time to ensure timely and safe travel in country and winter road conditions.

In conclusion, our research findings show that while formal home support services may not be as readily available in rural as in urban areas, and there are issues specific to working, living and receiving service in a rural context, rural places can still be supportive to ageing in place. Indeed, the accounts of residents of rural communities describe high levels of family/friend support and direct assistance to older people in need. The presence or absence of formal services is not the sole indicator of the social vitality of rural communities, nor the only indicator of whether rural areas are indeed good places in which to grow old.

Note

[1] Homecare work involves a wide variety of workers with different levels of training and qualifications. They include nurses, care managers, social workers, physiotherapists, occupational therapists and home support workers. Most homecare workers fall within the category of home support, and are often 'unregulated' workers who provide non-professional services in the form of personal assistance with daily activities, such as bathing, dressing, grooming and light household tasks. In the opening quote to this chapter, the older woman describes some of the types of home support tasks such as getting lunch, dinner and 'putting you to bed'. The individuals who provide this support are variously known as home support workers, personal care workers, community health workers, home helps and homemakers (Martin–Matthews, 2007). In 2001, an estimated 32,000 home support workers provided 70–80% of the homecare needs of Canadian homecare recipients. This included both personal care (bathing, toileting, grooming and so on) and work related to instrumental needs (for example, food preparation, cleaning, laundry and so on) (Home Care Sector Study Corporation, 2003).

SIX

Respite for rural and remote caregivers

Neena L. Chappell, Bonnie Schroeder and Michelle Gibbens

Introduction

The complexity of the concept 'rural' is well recognised, whether the focus is on size, the sociocultural or the sociopolitical. Even size, arguably the easiest descriptor to deal with, eludes consensus; government definitions range from sizes of 300 to 300,000 (Woods, 2005). In addition, the traditional image of rural as a pastoral setting with conservative values, idyllic slower-paced lives, close-knit communities with flourishing family values and connection to land and locality has been replaced with an acknowledged heterogeneity among rural settings (Giarchi, 2006b). Many aspects of rural communities are now contentious. They vary in terms of distance from urban centres where some are so proximate that they are in the urban shadow; social support may be strong or the exodus of young people might leave a dearth of informal assistance; and longstanding land use and values might be stable or in flux, affected by immigration of both urbanites and mobile transients. Rural communities are undergoing fundamental shifts in their very nature (Woods, 2006).

A number of features nevertheless characterise this environment: small populations, low density of population, distance from urban centres, monetary and time costs for travel, and a relative lack of formal transportation, healthcare and other services (CIHI, 2006). The role of family supports is less clear because of contrasting images of rural settings as supportive and expressed concerns, especially for an older population, that the exodus of youth leaves behind a serious lack of family support. In this chapter, attention is directed towards an area of intersection of formal and informal care for older adults in rural areas through an examination of respite.

While the concept of respite is a professional term (Brody et al, 1989), the need for a break is one of caregivers' most frequently expressed needs (Stoltz et al, 2004). Most of the research on caregiver respite has been conducted in urban settings although the concept is equally applicable in rural settings. Arguably, it is of greater importance in those rural settings where youth exodus has left behind fewer others to provide care for older adults. Three different rural regions in Canada offer insight into supporting caregivers in their individual and unique needs for a break in ways that caregivers themselves want. These communities offer innovative formal programmes that facilitate a break for caregivers. This chapter reports on six guiding principles derived from information shared by project personnel: acknowledging caregivers as partners in care, raising awareness of caregiver issues, networking to engage and maintain the interest of key stakeholders, developing advisory steering committee structures, encouraging caregiver leadership, and building community capacity.

Respite or having a break

While having a break is something we often do in our day-to-day lives, whether providing care or not, formal services are not typically involved. An exception is formal respite services for caregivers to older adults. In developed nations, three services are usually offered: sitter-attendant services in the home to allow the caregiver to undertake non-caregiving tasks; adult day care or day hospital where the older adult is taken for a few hours one or two days a week; and respite care beds in a facility where the older adult stays for a few to several days. Research evaluating respite services is inconclusive, some reporting beneficial effects for the caregiver often in terms of satisfaction with the services (Gottlieb, 1995; Zarit, 1998), some reporting no benefits (McNally, 1999; Lee and Cameron, 2004).

This literature has been criticised on both conceptual and methodological grounds. Conceptually, respite is a break from caregiving, not a service per se, although both service providers and researchers have de facto defined it as such. Therefore, evaluations of respite have been criticised for methodologically designing studies as if respite is a service rather than an outcome. They typically compare caregivers before and after using respite services or compare caregivers using respite services with those using another service or not using respite services (Chappell et al, 2001; McGrath et al, 2006). There is a design flaw in these studies: caregivers not using respite services may be experiencing a break from another source such as the hospitalisation of the older adult, the visit of children and so on. The designs do not account for the fact that caregivers can receive a break from sources other than service receipt. Conversely, caregivers may use respite services but still be concerned and thinking about the care recipient and not experience a break (Watts and Teitelman, 2005).

Through in-depth qualitative interviews, caregivers themselves have told us what having a break means to them (Chappell et al, 2001). A typology containing six meanings was derived, and then confirmed among a random sample of 250 caregivers to older persons. The largest category is *stolen moments* wherein the caregiver spoke of brief periods within their daily routine away from the tasks of caregiving. They are moments 'stolen' to take a bath, walk the dog, shop for groceries, typically activities that have to be done. Almost half (48%) referred to this type of break. The next most common category (18%) refers to having a *relief* from caregiving, to obtain physical and mental distance from the role. This is different from a *mental/physical boost* (11%) in which caregivers become totally absorbed (physically, mentally or both) in an activity. Other meanings include minimising the importance of needing a break, connecting with other people and an angst-free (happy or content) care recipient. Interestingly, the meaning of having a break does not vary by gender or social class.

This study confirmed the notion of respite as an outcome rather than a service and demonstrated the importance of caregivers' own meanings when thinking about respite. It points to a lack of synergy between caregivers and service providers on this issue. It was recommended that service providers ask caregivers what a break means to them and how they can best receive one that is meaningful. In asking caregivers themselves to define having a break, this study departed from others that focus on particular types of breaks such as McGrath and colleagues' (2000) in-depth study examining the experience of being physically and mentally engaged or Strang's (2001) study of respite as personal freedom, the essence of which is a state of mind in which the caregiver is mentally distant from the caregiving role.

While no research is available on implementing respite as an outcome, we know that caregivers are a heterogeneous group with differential needs (Cox, 1998) and abilities to utilise services, both of which must be taken into account when considering their needs for a break. Gilmour (2002) also notes the importance of the caregiver's perception of the service being offered. Caregivers can hold any number of beliefs that make it difficult to accept services that will provide them with a break: feeling selfish about needing a break; believing only they can provide the care; negative reactions of the care recipient when the caregiver is away; believing that others are reluctant to provide care; believing the person is not safe with others (Teitelman and Watts, 2004). As noted by Strang and Haughey (1999), caregivers must recognise their need for respite, give themselves permission to take it and have the social support available to facilitate it.

There is even less research on how to assist caregivers in having a break in rural locations. Older adults living in rural areas may be as integrated into family and non-family support systems as are those in urban areas. However, children and neighbours often live farther away; this can translate into practical assistance that is not readily available. Transportation is a major need, magnified by the fact that it may be less accessible due to geographic dispersion of people, facilities and services (Joseph and Martin-Matthews, 1993). Rural areas typically have fewer services, especially community-based services, including fewer if any formal respite services (Barber, 1998; Hong, 2006).

We now have a greater understanding of respite or a break as an outcome experienced by caregivers. It is not a service. We also know something about the diverse needs of caregivers and about many of the characteristics of rural areas that might affect the implementation of a programme to assist caregivers in taking a break. However, we know little about how to implement a programme within rural settings that defines respite as an outcome that must be individualised for each caregiver. We turn now to a discussion of three rural regions that have been experimenting with such a mandate.

The rural context

The three demonstration projects discussed here received targeted, time-limited financial assistance from a non-governmental funder. They were charged with being responsive, flexible and empowering to caregivers, giving them a choice in what was offered and a voice in determining their own needs. They were to operate differently from current practice, characterised as restrictive and system-defined. Project reports and semi-structured interviews with representatives from each project (a project manager, project co-coordinator and volunteer project co-coordinator) were analysed for common themes in terms of challenges and successes within their experiences. A joint teleconference with these project representatives was conducted to confirm (or refute) emerging themes. All quotes in this chapter come from these consultations. Six common principles emerged from these data. We start with a brief discussion of the context within which the programmes were implemented.

These regions differ considerably from one another: the *Seniors Resource Centre of Newfoundland and Labrador* has a province-wide mandate to support caregivers. Newfoundland and Labrador is Canada's most eastern coastal province with 370,501 square kilometres and a population of 512,930 in 2001. Extreme cold and significant amounts of snowfall limit the ability to travel in winter. Unemployment is high (13% compared with a Canadian average of 6%). Almost half of caregivers reside in communities of 5,000 or fewer. This area can be characterised as many small communities spread over great geographic distance.

Family Caregivers of Pictou County, Nova Scotia is a rural community caregiver-support programme in Nova Scotia (also on the east coast of Canada). The county has a population of 48,000 and is approximately 8,468 square kilometres. It consists of one larger community of approximately 10,000 people, and four smaller towns with surrounding rural communities and one First Nations reserve. Although the furthest south of the three regions, the county nevertheless experiences very cold temperatures and large amounts of snowfall, restricting travel in winter. Over half of the people live in rural areas. The area can be characterised as a central community with periphery towns and rural areas.

The Pauktuutit Inuit Women of Canada implemented respite for caregivers in six remote northern fly-in communities with no road access. Harsh Arctic winter conditions mean that residents cannot leave their communities for months at a time. Built space is scarce, with multiple generations often living in one household and no community space (halls or community centres). The population of each community is 550 to 1,500 people; each is 2,000 to 3,000 kilometres from a major urban centre. The first language of the communities is not English but the healthcare system is English-speaking, posing additional challenges. Cultural differences are also evident. The concepts of caregiving and caregiver support were new to Inuit people – Pauktuutit had to develop symbols and terms to communicate these ideas, not because residents were not providing care but rather that this work was not acknowledged. This area can be characterised as geographically isolated fly-in communities with language and culture different from the English-speaking Canadian majority.

The three regions also share many characteristics. All are rural with the geographic constraints that typify this environment. All experience winters with extremely cold temperatures and significant amounts of snowfall, albeit to differing degrees, that limit the ability to travel within and beyond the immediate area during winter. Such weather conditions restrict caregivers' ability to leave their home for support, as well as opportunities for advisory group or network meetings to advance respite initiatives during these months.

All have relatively small populations and significant distances from larger centres, translating into a lack of availability of the formal supports that caregivers and their care receivers require. All interviewees cited few formal services and a lack of awareness of the programmes that did exist; resources specifically for caregivers are virtually non-existent. It is common to travel significant distances for supports that would be readily available in urban communities such as support groups and support and education programmes offered by voluntary health agencies or healthcare facilities. Travel for medical appointments is commonplace and is both costly and time-consuming. The lack of public transportation aggravates the situation. In some instances caregivers may not be able to access services at all. For example, replacement care services that are frequently available through community-based homecare programmes and long-term care facilities in urban communities often do not exist in such rural communities.

This geographic isolation impacts caregivers' ability to experience respite – whether in northern Canada where they cannot leave the community for months at a time or further south in more temperate rural regions where travelling to an evening support group may entail a six-hour commitment involving late-night driving on isolated and icy roadways. Consequently, communities are looking for solutions that offer caregivers opportunities closer to home.

With fewer people come other challenges for implementing and sustaining respite for caregivers. One is a limited pool of human resources for developing opportunities for respite, whether volunteer or paid. There is also typically a lack of physical space for bringing people together. Communal or public spaces are often unavailable for meetings or other kinds of group activities. Size also means that people know one another. While this can be an asset, it can also raise concerns around confidentiality and privacy in a small or isolated community, preventing caregivers from asking for help or limiting their use of services. It also means that the boundaries between volunteer and other roles are often blurred, leading to increased expectations of those providing support. (See Chapter Five by Joanie Sims-Gould and Anne Martin-Matthews for a related discussion of the difficulties for paid homecare workers of maintaining boundaries between their employment and neighbour/friend roles.) Because relationships often extend back several generations they can be foundational for collaboration or for barriers.

Thus, despite the geographic differences among the three projects, they share common features by virtue of their rurality. These include: small populations, low-density populations, geographical distance compounded by climate, lack of formal services and limited human resources. These commonalities are part of the physical and social context within which the challenges of providing support for a break are implemented.

Implementing a programme to support caregivers in rural communities

Within the context noted above, each project set about to implement respite as an outcome. Looking back on their experiences, six foundational principles, listed earler in the chapter, were identified that were enacted by all projects to facilitate respite. All believe that caregivers themselves must recognise their need for a break, allow themselves to take it and be able to access the social support to enable it. First, they all began by *acknowledging caregivers as partners in care*. This was especially challenging in Pauktuutit where there were no words for the concepts of caregiving and respite.

Part of acknowledging caregivers as partners is accepting that care recipients' needs must be met and that caregivers bring knowledge of care recipients that must be recognised and respected. This is consistent with other research pointing to the unselfish concern caregivers have for care recipients, typically ignoring their own needs (Chappell, 1998). The message for formal care providers is to ensure proper care for the older adult if they expect caregivers to attend to their own needs.

Second, all projects consider *raising awareness of caregiver issues* as essential to their success. Raising awareness that providing care can be taxing and the care provider might want and need a break is necessary because caregiving is often an unidentified and unacknowledged cultural expectation. Interviewees noted that, in their experience, caregivers do not self-identify. All projects use a multiple component strategy with two main objectives: to raise awareness about the challenges facing caregivers and their related needs for support, and to encourage caregivers to self-identify and ask for support. It is important for non-caregivers to recognise that their friends or family who are providing care might benefit from being asked proactively what help they need and being given an opportunity to have a break and/or support.

Each project emphasises different methods, choosing ones they believe are most effective. Newfoundland uses a telephone Caregiver Line, print media and an annual provincial Caregiver Week. Nova Scotia uses an outreach model to identify caregivers. Pauktuutit uses radio to promote the issues as well as t-shirts and posters. However, consciousness-raising alone is not enough.

A third principle involves *networking to engage and maintain the interest of key stakeholders* such as healthcare and social services providers, community groups and government representatives. Specific strategies vary: Newfoundland and Pauktuutit use media campaigns to convey their messages across large geographic areas. Public radio is a key source of information for those in more isolated communities where radio call-in shows are utilised to spread the message. For the far north, a series of public service announcements was developed and aired by a public broadcaster free of charge. Other activities include distribution of promotional items incorporating a visual identity for the caregiver respite initiative.

Partnerships with diverse stakeholders are essential. The fourth principle posited that *advisory or steering committee structures* are necessary for developing a community response to caregivers' needs because they engage a diverse range of stakeholders in advising and directing the projects' activities. Partners include healthcare and social services workers, faith organisations, voluntary sector organisations, family, friends, caregivers and former caregivers, drawing on a broad base. These partnerships facilitate recognition of the importance of both paid services and unpaid supports. Trust is essential to the formation of partnerships and requires "time, it does not just happen". As stated by an interviewee, "you need to get people to know your face before you bring your issues forward".

The fifth principle embraces *caregiver leadership*. Caregivers or former caregivers are active partners in all initiatives, voicing the concerns and needs of caregivers. Caregivers' involvement in the advisory structures ensures that activities will be useful. Their leadership and participation also generates a passionate commitment among caregivers themselves and other partners to the goal of enabling caregivers to experience respite. One example is spearheaded by two former caregivers who contribute thousands of volunteer hours to awareness-raising and coordination of responses to meet individual caregivers' self-identified needs. Their commitment has meant that caregiver issues have a high profile within the community and in formal healthcare planning processes. All projects report similar leadership and impacts in their communities.

Each of the projects focuses on the sixth principle of *building community capacity* to support caregivers. (See also Jacquie Eales et al, Chapter Eleven, for a discussion of elements of age-friendly rural communities.) Energy and resources are not directed to developing formal programmes requiring intensive resources to sustain them. Rather, efforts are directed towards engaging diverse partners in processes to identify needs for which creative solutions can be developed and sustained as necessary to support many caregivers. As one of the interviewees said, "[it is] using what you got and what the caregivers' got. It is not necessarily creating new programmes and services, but it is working with what is out there.... What works in one community does not necessarily work in another". For example, the province of Newfoundland and Labrador focuses on partnership building and collaboration in the creation of eight regional caregiver networks. The networks identify their own activities for enabling caregivers to experience respite (such as caregiver retreats, education and support opportunities). Project personnel work with government to highlight the needs of caregivers at policy tables. Pauktuutit, on the other hand, faced with limited communal space for gatherings, uses the radio, small meetings in homes close to the care receiver and linkages to larger community issues.

Importantly, strategies to create opportunities for respite need not be expensive – 'caregivers ask for little'. Solutions, however, need to be multifaceted because the same strategies do not work for everyone. Respite is about 'making it work' for individual caregivers, their support networks and their communities. This requires creativity and flexibility in responding to individual needs, understanding the caregiver's context of family, friends, neighbours, volunteers and healthcare and social services. Resources to provide breaks must fit this individualised context. For example, respite options might focus on the needs of the care recipient to allow time for the caregiver to engage in their own activity – a home visitor to stay with the recipient so the caregiver can work in the garden. Alternately, respite options may focus on the social needs of the caregiver so that they can interact with their friends. In another case, a caregiver wanted to take her husband swimming once a week as he had done prior to his dementia. The project matched his wife-caregiver with a volunteer who drove and went swimming with them each week. The caregiver began to feel better about herself and her relationship with her husband and started doing more for herself, including accessing services, bringing family in for support and going to exercise classes. After her husband entered a nursing home, she began supporting another caregiver, a relationship that has blossomed into a support network of four current and former caregivers.

The six principles for facilitating respite are foundational, an ongoing guide in the provision of a break to caregivers. Embracing caregivers as partners; raising awareness of caregiving issues among both caregivers themselves, their family and friends and the general public; networking and engaging stakeholders; creating advisory structures inclusive of key stakeholders; caregiver leadership; and building community capacity that encourages creativity and individualising support – these are all necessary elements for any community that supports breaks for caregivers.

Rurality, however, impinges on the implementation of specific strategies using these principles. Since there are fewer formal service options in rural areas, communities rely almost exclusively on family, friends and other volunteers to create the options, either individually or collectively. Weather conditions in these particular communities impact on access to services offering replacement care, creating barriers to successful provision of support. Caregivers may require transportation to travel distances for attending meetings which ensure partnership and leadership; networking and engaging stakeholders may require more use of telecommunications. Finally, the same people may play several roles. These specifics of context, however, do not obviate the importance of the general principles.

Providing a break

Within an environment reflective of these principles, how is a break provided? Projects facilitate breaks by organising others to take over tasks that caregivers normally do. This provides an opportunity for caregivers to engage in other activities. One event, called 'A Day Away', offers educational programmes, retreats, meals and replacement care. The experience has forged relationships between caregivers and their support networks. For some, respite is not about leaving the person for whom they provide care, but opportunities to participate in rituals or traditions that connect them with others. The ability to stop and have a cup of tea and bannock, a traditional bread of the North of Canada, is an example. The ability to recharge through this simple act provides relief. Volunteers sometimes take the person requiring care for a drive, fishing, to a men's church group or the local coffee shop to visit other retired men in their community.

Although different activities and people are involved in providing the caregiver with a break, the activity itself is not respite. Whether a caregiver receives a break depends on their frame of mind. An interviewee said, "it is a feeling that they are not trapped, that they have options, they need supports". It can refer to 'coming out of isolation' or a 'sense of connectedness'. It includes an emotional break; it is about how the caregiver feels, it includes feeling connected and supported.

How do project personnel know caregivers are experiencing a break? An interviewee said, "You hear the feedback almost immediately. You hear the personal stories first-hand. You see the smiles in the faces. [You] see the changes." Caregivers speak about feeling less isolated knowing this resource and relationship can be accessed.

Sustainability

After three to six years, all projects find it necessary to remind caregivers to give themselves permission to experience respite and that respite is as much or more a 'state of mind' as actively doing other things. Despite a willingness to respond to the needs of caregivers because of pre-existing relationships in rural areas, often community members still do not offer help spontaneously because they are either unaware that the caregiver needs support or they lack knowledge about how they can help and are reluctant to ask the caregiver directly. Rather, they respond when called to action to support caregivers generally or are asked a specific request for a particular caregiver.

That is, a concerted effort is required to generate the response. Participants have multiple commitments competing for their limited time; 'volunteer fatigue' is a concern. 'Compulsory volunteerism' is noted in Chapter Eight where Julia Rozanova et al describe a situation in which people in small communities feel obliged to contribute because there are so few people available to help. Communication with partners, awareness-raising, travel, teleconferencing and making linkages between resources and needs, either at the individual or community level – these must be ongoing to sustain caregiver support initiatives. Adequate continuing funding is required.

Conclusion

This chapter has examined the implementation of 'respite as an outcome, not a service' in three rural regions of Canada from the point of view of the project personnel working within formal organisational structures. No data were available directly from caregivers themselves. Six principles were derived from the experiences of implementing a respite programme that could be individualised to needs identified by caregivers themselves. All six were foundational, providing guidance for the programmes throughout their operations. They add to our knowledge about how to ensure that rural places are good places to grow old.

While the principles themselves might be applicable outside of rural settings, the distinctiveness of rurality is evident. The lack of formal services means a necessary reliance on family and friends with long histories with one another. Creativity and flexibility, together with the pre-existing informal, less structured and non-hierarchical nature of long-term relationships in rural areas, are considered key to the success of the programmes and to their potential for sustainability. Pre-existing relationships, however, can also be barriers if the history between the people has not been positive. In addition, small populations mean fewer people to share the load. Burnout can happen to caregivers and their helpers alike.

Is growing old in rural areas good? That depends. For some, the answer is yes; for some, no doubt, it is no. How do we ensure a 'yes' response? One of the interviewees expressed it well: "People on the ground in communities finding solutions to daily problems and ideas to make communities a better place". The three projects discussed here are examples of such an approach to supporting caregivers. They teach us much about successfully mounting such programmes in rural areas as well as some of the challenges and pitfalls. They do not, however, address the question of the boundaries between state and family care, the question of who 'should' be providing care or how much care is reasonable for family and friend caregivers to provide.

SEVEN

Ageing, disability and participation

Janet Fast and Jenny de Jong Gierveld

Meaningful participation and social integration in society have been shown to contribute to ageing well. Both cross-sectional and longitudinal research have linked social participation to positive outcomes including quality of life (Silverstein and Parker, 2002), emotional well-being (Lee and Russell, 2003), functional independence (Unger et al, 1997) and lower morbidity and mortality rates (Menec, 2003). Importantly, social participation is seen to lead to social embeddedness – the evaluation of one's social situation as one of a satisfying interconnectedness and belonging. Some researchers have argued that involvement in social organisations via volunteer work, church attendance, participation in cultural, recreational and other associations, and donating, provide pathways to greater social embeddedness (van Tilburg et al, 1998; Broese van Groenou, 2007). Others have argued that participation is a necessary but insufficient precursor to social embeddedness, which requires that contact with others be meaningful, pleasant and based on positive relationships (de Jong Gierveld and Hagestad, 2006; de Jong Gierveld et al, 2006).

An assumption about rural communities addressed throughout this book is that they foster participation and a strong sense of social integration of residents through volunteer opportunities that are transparent and compelling, proximate families and friends who support each other, inclusive social organisations and rural identities that are fostered through lifelong linkages to people and place. In deconstructing these notions, authors have challenged such assumptions, pointing to the tremendous diversity among rural people and places. For example, Jacquie Eales et al (Chapter Eleven) show that engagement in volunteer activities can provide wonderful opportunities for retirement in-migrants to develop links to their new communities or for longstanding residents to give back to communities that have been supportive to them. However, in places that lack service infrastructure and have a small pool of people providing unpaid necessary services, there is a sense of 'compulsory volunteerism'. Similarly, while some older adults thrive on the social connections fostered through involvement, others are not joiners and do not wish to be. Further, Thomas Scharf and Bernadette Bartlam (Chapter Ten) present compelling data on how rural communities can be the antithesis of places for social embeddedness, with some residents unable to benefit from, or participate in, the resources in their communities because of social exclusion.

In this chapter we further address these assumptions, focusing on processes of ageing and disability in rural and urban contexts. We draw on distinctions made by Tamara Daly and Gordon Grant in Chapter Two between normative processes of ageing and the changing demands inherent in ageing with a disability. We set this discussion within an exploration of whether rural and urban contexts are more or less likely to facilitate participation and social inclusion of those who are ageing with or without disabilities.

Age and disability are often assumed to restrict the ability to participate fully in social networks and the broader community. These potential restrictions are of increasing concern as growing numbers of people with severe disability are surviving into old age (Janicki and Ansello, 2000; Tryssenaar and Tremblay, 2002). In addition, the population aged 80 and over – those most likely to acquire age-related chronic illness or disability – is growing faster than any other age group (Martel and Malenfant, 2007). Social participation of older adults and social participation of adults with disabilities have been typically studied separately. However, as Daly and Grant discuss in Chapter Two, a lifecourse approach to adults with disabilities incorporates both normative transitions as a result of ageing and those that may occur as the result of the onset of disabilities at any age. The personal and policy challenges faced by older adults and adults with disabilities overlap on issues such as the ability to live independently and to have access to information, transportation, housing, social services and adequate income (Priestley and Rabiee, 2002). Pitkeathley (2007) asserts that such an approach is critical in order to avoid the pitfalls of competition between ageing and disability groups.

In this chapter we also draw on assumptions from Chapter One in which Norah Keating and Judith Phillips set out the importance of community context in creating opportunities and constraints for individuals' community participation. The World Health Organization (WHO, 2002) states that the ability to participate comes from the interaction of people with the contexts in which they live. Participation may be constrained by several factors including health conditions and environmental and personal factors that may change over time so that the extent and patterns of participation vary across the lifecourse. In turn, these patterns may be differentially related to disability at different lifecourse stages, and to the nature of the community environments within which people live (WHO, 2002). Given the focus of this book, we emphasise rural compared to urban community contexts.

In the face of population ageing and increasing levels of disabilities, policy makers and practitioners are now emphasising communities as key sources of collaboration, self-help and capacity building in meeting the challenges of providing services to an ageing population (Kloseck et al, 2006). Kloseck et al go so far as to suggest that younger-old residents should support their frailer older-old neighbours so that they can remain in the community. While such exhortations may provide an impetus for ongoing engagement and participation, little is known about whether quality and meaningfulness of participation and interaction with others influence the sense of embeddedness of adults as they grow older.

It is often assumed that urban environments are more supportive of those with disabilities than rural environments. Geographic dispersion and isolation, accessibility challenges due to the natural and built environments, lack of public transport, and an emphasis on individual responsibility and independence can make it more difficult for those with activity limitations to engage in rural communities (Kent et al, 2000; Tryssenaar and Tremblay, 2002). Indeed Gething (1997) demonstrates that living with a disability and living in a rural community constitutes a 'double disadvantage' when it comes to receipt of services, many of which are critical to achieving full social participation and inclusion. In contrast, it is sometimes assumed that rural communities are more closely knit and supportive than urban communities and therefore more inclusive, perhaps compensating for lack of service infrastructure (Julia Rozanova et al, Chapter Eight).

In this chapter we examine the interplay of age and disability, and of urban and rural location, in determining social participation. We further examine the role of social participation in shaping subjective feelings of social integration. More specifically, we ask whether disability is a relevant determinant of social participation across stages of the adult lifecourse; whether urban versus rural residency is a relevant determinant of social participation for those with and without disability across the lifecourse; and whether social participation influences people's sense of social integration.

To answer these questions we draw on both quantitative and qualitative Canadian data. Statistics Canada's *General Social Survey on social engagement*, conducted in 2003, is a nationally representative telephone survey that includes information on participation in a variety of activities. In this chapter we use a subsample of adults aged 25 and over to examine engagement in four specific types of social participation: volunteering; helping others; belonging to social organisations; and donating money or goods. Data were also collected on whether respondents experienced any activity limitations at work, at home or in leisure and other settings, and on their perceptions of how connected they felt to their home communities.

Data from two qualitative studies were used to illustrate and elaborate on the quantitative findings. One study, conducted in three small rural Canadian communities, included in-depth interviews with older adults and other community stakeholders (Eales et al, 2006). The second study involved a series of focus group interviews on the participation and contributions of older adults and people with disabilities. Two of the six stakeholder groups interviewed are relevant to this chapter: urban community-dwelling older people and people with disabilities.

The first type of social participation we examined is volunteering. Volunteering is an important vehicle for social interactions between people and has been shown to have beneficial effects for quality of life for both the people served and the volunteers serving them (Wheeler et al, 1998). The survey data used in this chapter allow us to account for the time spent volunteering with youth groups, sports teams, churches, political parties and arts organisations. Membership in some of these groups can be rather passive: for example, Amnesty International, an influential organisation in Canada, has many members but only 10% of them are actively involved in campaigning for human rights (Quarter et al, 2003). Other volunteer activities are much more demanding in terms of time and energy: weekly involvement in church activities for younger and older church members, instruction, refereeing or scorekeeping for youth football or baseball clubs and so on. Frail older adults and other adults with disabilities are likely to find the latter type of engagement more challenging.

The second form of social participation – helping others – involves performing tasks for a family member, friend or neighbour. Tasks may include domestic work, home maintenance or outdoor work, transportation or running errands, childcare, teaching, coaching, giving practical advice or helping a person in some other way (Fast et al, 2006). As with work performed for volunteer organisations, providing direct help to others has been shown to enhance the well-being of the helper and those being helped. The work of Desrosiers et al (2004, 2005), among others, leads us to expect that there may be declines in this type of engagement with advancing age, but that declines will be steeper for those with disabilities.

The third type of social participation is membership in organisations oriented towards shared recreational, educational and/or cultural activities. Involvement in these formal organisations provides an opportunity for people to meet others with common interests and build new friendships, and in doing so broaden their social networks and their connections with other members of their community (Broese van Groenou, 2007). Formal organisations can be instrumental in building informal bonds that are connected with feelings of belongingness (van Tilburg et al, 1998; Broese van Groenou, 2007).

The fourth form of social participation – donating money or goods – is another indicator of involvement. It differs from the other domains in that donations are not geographically bound. However, donations are dependent on the willingness of people to support activities such as those that meet special needs of community members or towards other 'good works'. Dutch and other studies show that people with higher education levels and higher socioeconomic status are no more frequently involved in donating substantially to 'good works' than others, but they make larger donations (Schuyt and Gouwenberg, 2005). Nonetheless, among contributors, those with lower incomes contribute a higher proportion of their incomes (Hall et al, 2001). We expect that those who are embedded more strongly in their communities are more willing to contribute resources to charitable causes in order to guarantee the ongoing work of important communal activities. Because donations do not require physical or social engagement, they may be less influenced by age, disabilities or community context than other types of participation.

Age, disability and participation in urban and rural communities

We believe that it is important to distinguish age from disability. Disabilities may have their onset at any point in the lifecourse. For some, activity limitations are related to health or functional problems that started at birth or during early childhood. For others, activity limitations have later life onset. While there are higher risks of chronic health problems and disabilities with age, late-life disabilities are no more inevitable than are early-life health and functional abilities. In this chapter we use a typology of activity limitations across the lifecourse that allows us to examine the interplay between disability and age. It comprises eight categories of four age groups (22-44, 45-64, 65-74 and 75+), each with or without disabilities.

It should be noted first that, contrary to expectations, a higher proportion of respondents living in rural areas and small towns reported activity limitations than those living in larger urban centres. This finding may contradict conventional wisdom that rural communities are hostile to people with disabilities, driving them to gravitate towards urban living. It may be that people with disabilities do not leave rural communities despite the fact that rural environments are more limiting for them than for those without disabilities.

Volunteering

In investigating people's involvement in volunteering, we differentiate those who volunteer fewer than five hours per month from those who volunteer for five or more hours per month. Figure 7.1 shows that people of all ages, with and without activity limitations, in both urban and rural communities, volunteer. However, spending more than five hours per month on volunteer work is more common in rural than urban communities. One of the older adults interviewed in our rural study explains why this might be:

> 'We retired ... we came [to the community] in the spring of 2002. To get connected to people in the community ... was crucial for us because we didn't know anybody here. So we really had to plunge into different organisations.... It was very important to have the people contact ... we got involved in a lot of things.... One of the nice things about a small town is that you can get involved in things that you wouldn't get involved in a larger place because you don't have experience in them.'

When the interplay among age, disability and urban/rural location are examined, activity limitations are shown to be most constraining for the oldest respondents and for middle-aged people in rural communities. But activity limitations make little difference in the youngest groups: young adults in both urban and rural

Figure 7.1: Percentage volunteering by lifecourse phase: limitation status and rural versus urban communities (Canada, 2003)

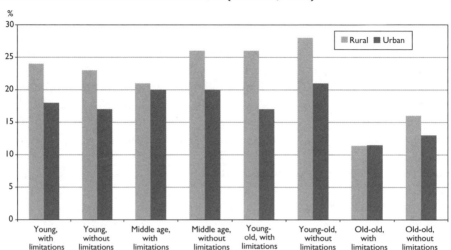

communities as well as middle-aged urban residents are equally likely to spend five hours or more on volunteer work each month whether they have activity limitations or not.

Some of the older adults who participated in our study of participation and contributions concur:

> '... it's a very tiny percentage of seniors that get involved and those are the healthy seniors. So if you can stay active and you can stay and participate, that's great. But if you are no longer able to do that, once you get sick, you drop out of the picture and you get forgotten.... Even ... healthy seniors are now themselves getting sick and getting older and it's harder for them to be doing or participating in all the activities that they have been participating in.'

Some observe quite the opposite. An older interviewee explains that in small rural communities, scarcity of young residents, perhaps due to out-migration to find employment, may account for our finding showing that volunteering more than five hours a month is more common among older people in rural communities than in urban ones:

> 'But I belong to a fire department as well, and uh, when I was mentioning before about volunteering, they tried [bringing] younger people out too, and there just isn't that many young people around.... It's kind of understandable in that way ... it's a challenge to get the younger people. I know that seniors that live in a small town like this,

seem to do more than, than like uh, my grandparents that live in the
city. They carry a lot of the load.'

Helping others

When we looked at the number of tasks with which respondents helped others,
we found a similar pattern to the one described above for volunteering. Rural
residents are more intensely involved in helping others than are those in urban
areas, regardless of age or presence of activity limitations. However, there are clearer
age differences in the extent of involvement in helping others. The average number
of tasks done for others declines steadily across the lifecourse. Young adults are by
far the most intensely involved in helping others. Middle-age adults help to a lesser
extent, the young-old somewhat less again and the old-old help with the fewest
tasks. But the contributions of those older adults who do help remain important,
as illustrated by this statement by an older woman focus group participant:

> 'My mother has made, oh probably 75 afghans for kids in our family
> and they're absolutely beautiful. She's taught kids how to crochet. She
> doesn't go out and do a lot of things. She's now 95 and she's still good
> in her head. She's still working on an afghan. I mean her contribution
> isn't in volunteer activities, it's in the people she meets and befriends,
> the things she does for her kids.'

Membership in community organisations

Rural residents not only participate more in volunteer work and provide more
direct assistance to others, they also belong to more community organisations
than urban residents. This pattern holds across lifecourse stages and disability
status, with the exception of adults without activity limitations in the earliest
stage of the lifecourse. There are striking differences between those with and
those without activity limitations. Respondents without limitations participate
in more organisations than those with limitations, regardless of lifecourse stage or
location of residence. Membership in community organisations is lowest among
the old-old, but belonging to a church, service organisation, art cooperative or
the like is nonetheless important to their quality of life, as illustrated by this older
rural resident:

> 'I kind of look forward to this [church suppers] 'cause you meet
> people and it's, I usually take the money at the door, and things like
> that. Keeps me going, it's good to be in a group, you know.... If my
> sister can't make it to church, one of them will come and get me …
> even our organist will come and get me.'

In sum, rural residents participate more than their urban counterparts in three of the four domains examined: volunteering, helping others and membership in community organisations. Only in making donations, a form of social participation that is not geographically constrained, is participation equally common among those living in rural and those living in urban communities. Similarly, involvement in volunteering, helping others and membership in community organisations declines in the latest stages of life, and activity limitations are most constraining with respect to participation in volunteering and helping work later in the lifecourse. Overall, old-old adults with activity limitations participate least in their local communities.

For many, decreased physical capacities in later life likely explain the decline in involvement, since activity limitations are found to have greater impact later in life. As an older woman focus group participant put it:

> '… not everybody has the type of energy you need to go, to reach out to others, to do all these kinds of things. Some people are just, have so many interior problems, that they really can't.'

Others clearly feel that they have done their part and are now pursuing their own interests – although not entirely without feeling guilty about it. One older focus group participant reported having done a great deal of volunteer work in the past, as well as caring for both of her parents when they were old. She was now engaged in pursuits for her own enjoyment:

> 'I think we all have some sense of obligation. I don't know if it's innate or whether it's something to do with our upbringing, but we feel some, that we ought to help out if we can. And I'd guess I'd have to say that at this point in my life, I'm in my 70s, that I feel a little bit guilty because I'm not helping out, but really I'm having such a good time.'

Activity limitations may have less impact on the volunteer work of younger adults because it provides a source of satisfaction that they are unable to obtain from paid work because of a lack of employment opportunities. One young man with schizophrenia who participated in a focus group of people with disabilities in a large urban centre reported that:

> '… volunteer organisations are one of the few people who accept me as I am. As I said I'm looking for paid work, I've gone all about giving out resumés and stuff and … I explain to them that my experience is volunteer and I haven't gotten anywhere. At least the volunteers at the [name of hospital], they accepted me and there's a lot of satisfaction I get from the unpaid work. But you tend to do more volunteer work when you're in my situation because at least they accept you. They don't worry about your resumé or your experience. They accept you.'

Donating

The donation of money and goods as an aspect of social participation shows a very different pattern from participation in other domains. This form of social participation is largely independent of age, especially for those with activity limitations. If anything, slightly higher proportions of older people without activity limitations make charitable donations. There may be more financial capacity among these older adults who may have higher incomes and/or lower expenses than those without limitations.

Age, disability and social integration

Earlier we suggested that rural environments might make it easier, or harder, for those who live there to participate in their community. Our findings clearly support the former: rural residents participate more in three of the four domains we examined. We also noted that social participation has, in turn, been linked to social integration or embeddedness, and quality of life. Our data similarly show that being more intensely involved in the community goes hand in hand with more intense feelings of belonging to that community. Respondents' sense of being connected to the community is strongest among those who volunteer for more than five hours per month and for those who participate in more social organisations. As one older rural participant put it:

> 'If you want to live in a certain type of community, you have to make a contribution to making it that kind of community.... And to get involved is the way to do that.'

Since involvement in volunteering, helping others and membership in community organisations declines in later life, we might also have expected to find a similar decline in social integration. However, as Figure 7.2 shows, it is the oldest, not the youngest, respondents who felt most tightly connected to their communities. Perhaps the answer to this apparent contradiction lies in the fact that community connectedness is a long-term outcome of longstanding bonds within the community. The opportunity to be involved in volunteer work, helping others and/or social organisations in the early and middle stages of life by virtue of simply having lived longer might have positive outcomes for feeling embedded among young-old and even old–old residents. It is through bonds with fellow volunteers and colleagues in social organisations that new acquaintances and friends are met and informal bonds built that might be supportive for a long period of time (van Tilburg et al, 1998; Broese van Groenou, 2007).

Our survey data also show that older adults have larger networks of friends than younger adults, despite participating less in volunteering or helping work and belonging to fewer community organisations. Our findings also show that social network size is an important predictor of respondents' feelings of connectedness

Figure 7.2: Intensity of belongingness by lifecourse phase: limitation status and rural versus urban communities (Canada, 2003)

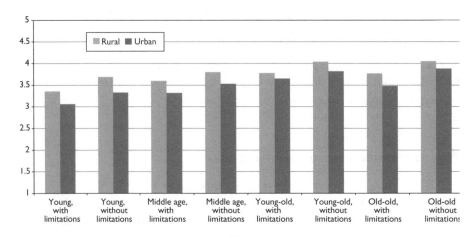

to their communities. Those interviewed in the course of the qualitative studies we are drawing on reported a wide range of activities with friends, without the structure of formal organisations. They called on friends for coffee or tea at home or at Tim Horton's (an iconic Canadian coffee and doughnut shop, popular for casual gatherings of friends, especially in small towns). They played poker or darts, dined out with friends and drove or accompanied friends and neighbours who needed help doing errands. And they celebrated birthdays and other special occasions and went to the theatre. As one older woman residing in a small rural town stated in response to a question about what made their rural community a good place to grow old: "Well, basically you're with people you know … if you decide to move to [the nearest large city] … new environment, you have to make friends". Another elaborated: "It can be very comforting when everybody knows you … you have friends here that I've only got to pick up the 'phone and tell them that I can't get out, or I don't feel well, [and] they'll be here in minutes".

In sum, while social participation is greatest among rural adults, participation appears to contribute similarly to the creation of feelings of social integration regardless of geographic location. Volunteering, helping others, donating and belonging to social organisations are instrumental in promoting feelings of being connected to the community.

Conclusion

We indicated earlier in this chapter that age and disability increasingly intersect, which may result in overlapping experiences and patterns of behaviour of older adults and adults with disability. Findings presented in this chapter support this proposition. There are differences in the absolute levels of participation and feelings of community connectedness between adults with and without disabilities, but the patterns across the lifecourse and by urban/rural location are remarkably similar.

Are rural communities good places to grow old, with or without a disability? The data reviewed in this chapter suggest that they are. Rural adults, with or without activity limitations, participated more in activities that have been connected to ageing well. Participation in these activities, in turn, was connected with more intense feelings of being connected with the community. Yet, as illustrated next in Chapter Eight, rural communities themselves are tremendously diverse in the ways in which they foster participation. The crude dichotomy between urban and rural location available in the survey data used in this chapter fails to account for such diversity. In Chapter Eight, Julia Rozanova et al begin to articulate the ways in which rural communities are differentially inclusive.

Our finding that rural communities appear to be more inclusive than urban ones even for adults with activity limitations also deserves further attention since it seems to fly in the face of arguments and evidence pointing to the 'double disadvantage' of living with a disability in rural communities. It may be that people in some rural communities feel pressured into volunteering because of social values, lack of local services, out-migration of younger residents, economic boom or bust and so on. Under such circumstances, participation in the volunteer sector may not be so beneficial (see Chapter Eight for further discussion of this proposition).

EIGHT

Participation in rural contexts: community matters

Julia Rozanova, Donna Dosman and Jenny de Jong Gierveld

Introduction

Extensive research has shown that social participation has positive associations with better health and well-being in later life. Individuals benefit when participation is meaningful to them (Chapman, 2005) and when personal relationships are formed or strengthened as a result of their engagement (de Jong Gierveld et al, 2006). Yet the ways in which older adults participate may make a difference in terms of whether participation has such positive outcomes. Participation that is freely chosen and is a good fit with one's identity and sense of self may foster positive outcomes (Chapman, 2005). Participation that is not satisfying or is done under duress may be less likely to contribute to ageing well.

Rural communities may be seen as good places for older adults to participate. It is believed that connections to others are easy to develop in these communities as they are small and often have stable populations where people have grown up and grown old together. There also is evidence that rural communities benefit greatly from the contributions of older adults (Liu and Besser, 2003) and in fact are quite dependent on their participation. For example, in some communities, the decline in primary industries like mining, fishing or forestry, or of family farms has led to out-migration of younger people and loss of service infrastructure (Horton, 2005). In others, a boom in resource-extraction industries or the development of retirement housing options in rural areas can generate in-migration to the degree that short-term infrastructure development may not keep pace with economic and population growth (Heather at al, 2005). In these contexts social participation is often seen as a vehicle for rural communities to reinvigorate a declining economy (Shortall, 2004) or to bridge the lack of infrastructure in the midst of an economic boom (Heather et al, 2005).

Rural communities rely on their citizens to support one another. Social participation now is seen as especially important in supporting the social fabric of the community, and in buttressing its service and public infrastructures (Bull, 1998; Shortall, 2004). Adults in mid to later life are seen as a reserve for this social participation. They are assumed to have more free time as their ties to paid work and childcare responsibilities are declining and thus are available for this community work (Herzog et al, 2002; Liu and Besser, 2003).

Overall, there seems to be a good fit between rural communities' needs for participation and the resources of older adults to meet these needs. Yet communities are not homogeneous in their opportunities for engagement. In some places, the opportunities for participation by older people may be limited due to their exclusion from social or material resources, or from services. Thomas Scharf and Bernadette Bartlam (Chapter Ten) note that exclusion may occur in rural communities with rapidly changing populations. Some older people in this situation may experience difficulties getting to know their new neighbours, and thus have restricted opportunities for social participation such as providing and receiving help from others. In communities experiencing an economic boom, exclusion from material resources may occur for segments of the population, like older adults on a fixed pension, whose income cannot keep pace with the rising costs of living. For them it may be impossible to afford out-of-pocket expenses associated with helping others and volunteering. Additionally, lack of public services such as public transportation can prevent participation in remote rural communities for older adults who do not drive their own vehicle.

In this chapter, we illustrate the ways in which characteristics of rural communities may or may not foster social participation of older rural residents. Social participation is an overarching concept used by researchers with regards to diverse social interrelationships (de Jong Gierveld et al, 2006). In this chapter we focus on two kinds of participation: helping others, especially providing care to dependent family members; and volunteer activities in formal organisations. These two types of participation illustrate different ways to engage with and contribute to the community. Helping others is based on individual connections and is personal, provided when a family member, friend or neighbour is in need. This participation relies on knowing when a person is in need and being available to provide support. Such contributions are often based on a sense of obligation and longstanding patterns of reciprocity. In contrast, volunteer activities are community oriented, and reliant on the existence of formal organisations and infrastructures rather than personal connections.

Community characteristics may influence these two types of participation in different ways. With respect to volunteering, communities may create situations that give rise to an organisation's existence and affect the level of resources available to it, such as membership, finances and physical space. In contrast, while helping others is predominantly based on personal connections, communities can create situations where people need help because of limited access to services, or where people have time to help others because there are limited employment opportunities. Depending on their characteristics, communities may present different opportunities to participate in helping others or volunteering, or pressures to do so.

This chapter follows Janet Fast and Jenny de Jong Gierveld's consideration in Chapter Seven of how age and disability influence levels and types of participation across the adult lifespan. The goal in this chapter is to better understand the influence that community characteristics may have on social participation. We draw on the same quantitative and qualitative datasets. From the Statistics Canada (2003) *General Social Survey on social engagement* we present findings from a subsample of rural adults aged 25 years and older. We examine how features of communities make a difference in levels of participation in helping others and in volunteering for younger and older rural residents as well as for women and men. (See Chapter Seven for measurement of these activities.) Quotes from a qualitative study of older adults and other community stakeholders conducted in three rural Canadian communities illustrate the influence of community characteristics on individuals' levels of social participation and their motivations for these contributions (Eales et al, 2006).

The influence of rural community characteristics on social participation

In rural Canada, a high proportion of community members helped someone out or volunteered in the past month: 74% of men and 72% of women helped others with various tasks, while 38% of men and 41% of women volunteered (unpublished data, Statistics Canada, 2003). In these next sections we discuss what is known about the influence of community characteristics on these two types of participation. We present findings that illustrate how they influence individuals to help others and volunteer. Only those characteristics that had a significant influence on an individual's level of social participation are presented. These are:

• remoteness from an urban centre
• population density
• changing population size
• community economic diversity
• proportion of older adults
• proportion of highly educated residents
• proportion of people who are members of a visible minority group.

Remoteness from an urban centre

Restricted access to a large urban centre is one characteristic of rural communities that may be associated with participation. Communities are often described as remote when people cannot take advantage of amenities found in urban centres because of distance or other barriers. Remote communities usually are small in population and lack the full set of basic financial, health and commercial services needed by all citizens.

There are no universal definitions of what constitutes remote. In rural Australia and Canada, remoteness is often associated with distance, exacerbated by harsh climate. It is not uncommon for the closest community to be several hundred kilometres away with limited access by road because of difficult terrain. Air transportation between these communities may be available but expensive. In contrast, rural communities in Europe may be remote when there are no urban centres within 50 kilometres. Lack of regular bus or train services between communities and low levels of vehicle ownership among older rural residents (Phillipson and Scharf, 2005) can mean that older adults in these areas also have problems gaining access to the services they need. In Chapter Six, Neena Chappell et al described a set of communities that differ greatly in their distance from larger centres but share problems with access to services and supports. Remote communities might be associated with higher levels of social participation because of the need for people to help a family member, friend or neighbour, or to compensate for lack of access to services. As Bonnie Dobbs and Laurel Strain show in Chapter Nine, social networks can be critically important to the mobility of older adults.

Findings from our research in rural Canada show that adults in remote communities do provide more help to family members, friends and neighbours. Men who live farthest from urban centres are more likely to help others by doing household work, providing transportation or running errands. These activities certainly could help compensate for lack of access to larger service centres. Driving someone to appointments at a distance may be particularly welcome for those who do not drive while running errands may be done in response to the need of a frail older person to have medications collected or groceries purchased.

Interviewer:	'People have talked about a sign that you have [in the window] for people from other communities [to] pick up prescriptions [for older adults who live there] to take back.'
Service provider:	'In the pharmacy setting ... seniors are an important part of your patient base.... When we can assist them in any way, we certainly do and with [one community] and [another community], where we send a lot of prescriptions. Someone will [come in and] say, anything for [another community]? And we send it, quite a number of those are going to seniors so ... they're getting their medication and don't have to drive in for it. We try our best.'

Population density

Population density refers to the average number of people living within a particular area. Less densely populated communities may not be able to provide the full range of public services such as fire fighting, a postal delivery service, post offices, healthcare and public transportation in part because the area is relatively large for the size of its property tax base (Woods, 2006). Where services are not available, residents must rely on others or on formal volunteer organisations. However, in very sparsely populated communities there may be fewer formal volunteer organisations due to the lack of membership or high overhead costs (Giarchi, 2006a), although such gaps can also create opportunities for or necessitate the development of new organisations to fill these gaps.

Findings from our research in rural Canada showed that the lower the population density in a community, the more time men spent on volunteer activities. In particular they were more likely to volunteer in religious affiliated groups, service clubs, sports organisations, school groups and neighbourhood and civic organisations. Men may be more involved because of the nature of some voluntary organisations. In sparsely populated rural Canadian communities, services such as fire fighting are almost exclusively provided by volunteers and the membership of many such voluntary organisations is predominantly male: "I've been involved in the fire department … for a few years [as a volunteer fire fighter].…There's a personal reason we're putting that fire out …".

Changing population age

Rural communities may experience changes in their populations that can affect opportunities or pressures to participate. In some regions of Western countries, agricultural communities and small single-industry towns are experiencing net population loss as young people move to urban centres for better employment prospects (Stockdale et al, 2000). This exodus leaves community organisations struggling to maintain their membership numbers. With the risk of continuing decline of their home community being real and immediate, residents may feel a heightened responsibility to contribute to and preserve their community (Salamon, 2003).

Conversely, some communities are experiencing population growth. Communities in regions that are experiencing economic booms and those near major urban areas may be attractive to young workers and their families because of job opportunities or a lower cost of living (Horton, 2005). In addition, communities with an attractive climate and recreational amenities may attract young retirees (Dahms and McComb, 1999; Horton, 2005; Chapter Eleven, this volume). A potential consequence of such population growth is a gap in services and infrastructure because the municipality is not able to keep pace with the population influx.

Findings from our research in rural Canada illustrate that women who live in communities where the population is declining spent considerably more time per month volunteering than women in stable or growing communities. An example from a community that has experienced such decline illustrates the effect of population decline on pressures to contribute. At one time in this community, the economy was strong, with a strong service base and a number of active and vibrant volunteer organisations. In recent decades the economy weakened, services were reduced and the population declined. In response, volunteer organisations mobilised to bridge the increasing scarcity of services. An older woman from such a community commented on the need for and the results of active involvement:

> 'That's my generation now [that constitutes the majority of volunteers], and they're worn out and tired. You know, they're doing the church volunteer work and they're running the Boy Scouts and doing the food bank, and they're doing this and that. I'm certainly old and worn out. [Laughs] Oh, I get a kick now and again. [But] the population is so few. The out-migration is terrible, has been for some time....'

In communities experiencing an increase in population, volunteer resources are more plentiful. Our findings show that men volunteered more hours and were more likely to spend time in civic organisations, school or neighbourhood groups that allowed them to use their abilities and skills while helping family members, friends or neighbours. Retirement communities may be particularly well served by young retirees with time and resources. As exemplified by the words of an older volunteer who lived in a retirement community:

> 'I have to say that one of the reasons I think that a programme like ours is so successful is its base of volunteers. We started out with 10 trained volunteers when we began. That has evolved over the years. We have about 160 volunteers at the moment.... We've never had to advertise for volunteers. They come to us.'

Volunteer opportunities may also serve as a means for newly arrived retirees to integrate into the community by meeting new people and developing their personal network:

> 'We were "imports" [into the community], and it was easy to get to know people when we [got] involved [in volunteer work]. I think it happened because of our situation. We were available. People knew we were available, so they could ask us if we would be interested in doing this and that, and that's what started from there.... [My wife] is treasurer at golf club, treasurer at church, coordinates Meals on Wheels, Eastern Star, Board of FCSS [Family and Community Support Services], Board of Big Country Education Consortium, Square Dance. I am involved with the Meals on Wheels, I play guitar and sing at church, look after rentals of rectory, do the lawn and [shovel] snow at church.'

Community economic diversity

The range and number of primary, manufacturing and service industries located in a community can affect opportunities for paid work, and the time and resources citizens have to volunteer and help others. The economy of some communities is focused on one or two primary industries such as farming and mining with a limited number of related service industries (Horton, 2005; Woods, 2006). These industries typically are male-dominated, providing few employment opportunities for women (Miller, 2004). Additionally, there are fewer other services, such as commercial, financial and healthcare services, available in these communities (Woods, 2006). The limited availability of positions in service industries where women typically work further restricts their opportunities for employment.

Limited employment opportunities for women may mean that their primary opportunity to make a contribution to their community is through helping other members of the community or via volunteer work. Our findings indicate that women who resided in communities with less diverse economies were more likely to provide help to family members, friends or neighbours. They provided transportation and ran errands, thus assisting others in accessing services outside of the community. These women were also more likely to help out by doing household tasks. An older woman in one rural Canadian community with a shrinking industrial base helped out her community members by providing transportation to distant services.

> 'At one time, it was a very vibrant town. There was a ferry across to the valley years ago.... [Now] very little industry ... the tourist industry ... that's about all that's left here ... you have to go out of town for any procedures. Transportation is nil. We used to have a train; that's gone. There's no bus anymore. I have in the last 10 years or so [I've] taken people to the airports or to doctors because there's nothing here.... A taxi to go out of town costs you a hundred dollars.... The people just don't have it, so if I'm here with somebody that needs to go and I'm not busy, then I don't mind taking them, you know.'

Women in less economically diverse communities potentially have more time to contribute to social participation. However, they did not spend more time volunteering. This may be due to lack of volunteer opportunities, which caused them to help others in their personal networks more than to engage in volunteer organisations.

Population of older adults

Some rural communities may have a higher proportion of older adults than others due to in-migration of older adults into retirement communities, or out-migration of younger people in search of better employment opportunities. Such communities may be well served since people in mid-life and older are more likely to make substantial contributions to their communities. Volunteer rates peak in middle age. On retirement the number of hours spent volunteering increases for those who already volunteer (Wilson, 2000; Erlinghagen and Hank, 2006). Only when infirmity or extreme old age sets in does the volunteer rate begin to fall (Wilson, 2000; Chapter Seven, this volume).

Findings from our research in rural Canada show that men in communities with high proportions of older adults spent more time volunteering in formal organisations. Older men were more likely to belong to service clubs, fraternal organisations or be affiliated with religious organisations. These types of organisations focus their efforts on helping those who are in need by developing service programmes designed to support and assist specific groups of people.

An older man from a rural Canadian community that has been experiencing out-migration of younger cohorts belonged to a service organisation called the Lions Club. He described a programme, which allows an older person to ring an emergency number by touching a button on a wrist bracelet. The service clubs offer this service:

> 'We as Lions install what they call a Lifeline, which helps seniors stay in their home.... Lifeline will call and say that they need a Lifeline installed at such-and-such a residence, and [another man] and I go in and install them. There's a charge for them, and if the person who requires one can't pay the full price, then between Lifeline and the Lions, we will put in some money to see that they ... make it happen.'

In contrast, women were more likely to provide help to family members, friends or neighbours by performing a greater number of other general tasks. One woman from a farming community where many farmers from the area around it retire helped out her friends by cooking for them: "I'll just make a big bunch of soup or I might make chicken pies ... and I'll take these to a couple of people I know that [could] use it". Another woman who lived in a retirement community helped out a friend by caring for his pet while he was having medical treatments in another community: "He's being treated for a tumour ... so we're looking after [his cat]".

Having a large cohort of older adults in a community can be beneficial to communities. However, as such cohorts age, the proportion of older people requiring assistance and the community organisations needing volunteers may surpass the ability of older adults in the community to provide assistance to them.

Proportion of highly educated residents

Having a post-secondary degree or diploma is an important predictor of volunteering and providing informal help to others (Wilson, 2000; Perren et al, 2003). It may be that individuals with a higher level of education are more aware of the needs of people in their social networks. They may also have a broader set of skills, which create opportunities to contribute. Certain types of volunteer activities such as positions on boards, advocacy groups and fundraising require a range of skills such as book-keeping, writing, public speaking, management or organisation. More highly educated people who have these skills may spearhead existing initiatives and establish new volunteer organisations, thus contributing to the development of volunteer opportunities in their community.

Findings from our research in rural Canada demonstrate that men and women who resided in communities with a high proportion of highly educated residents were more likely to volunteer in their communities. Men were more likely to help family members, friends or neighbours by informally teaching, providing advice or coaching, while women were more likely to help with other general tasks. Women in these communities also spent more time volunteering in a wide variety of community organisations such as union or political activities, civic or community associations, school or neighbourhood groups, and community activities including sports, recreation, culture or education.

As exemplified by the words of an older volunteer who resided in a retirement community with many retired professionals:

Volunteer: 'We started the first meal [on wheels], went out in February 1980.... And I was in on the planning of it, you know.... And it has worked beautifully. I'm very happy. I've been in, doing it ever since it started.'

Interviewer: 'Tell me, [name of respondent], you're so organised, what did you do before you started this?'

Volunteer: 'Oh, I was, you don't want to know this. I was executive secretarial supervisor at [a large company in Toronto]. The man that was the president owned nine other companies, and I was executive secretary, I was private secretary, to the executive president. We were doing the big [orders] for the government.'

This older woman further commented that she "got a heritage grant, and ... renovated and put in this kitchen", and since establishing the Meals on Wheels programme 25 years ago she has been its leader, coordinating the work of many community residents for whom the creation of this organisation provided volunteer opportunities:

'This is my work, getting the chart, and we meet here, and I have a chart pretty well figured out, and we figure out a menu. So, that they're getting different meals, and there's a different person who cooks every meal. I have about 150 volunteers.'

Proportion of residents from visible minority groups

Across the developed countries most people who are visible minorities live in urban areas, leaving rural communities with little racial mix among residents (Beshiri, 2004; Commission for Rural Communities, 2007b). In Canada, visible minorities are defined as 'persons, other than Aboriginal peoples, who are non-Caucasian in race or non-white in color' (Statistics Canada, 2005b). In rural communities, as elsewhere, these people may be 'vulnerable to prejudice, discrimination, and inadequate service provision' (Commission for Rural Communities, 2007b, p 2). Although racial diversity in rural areas is significantly lower than in urban areas, it may have serious impacts on the levels of social participation. While familiarity among rural community residents fosters social participation, increasing racial and ethno-cultural diversity in these areas may have the opposite effect, fostering distrust and 'othering' (Bull, 1998; Wenger, 2001b). Because few people who are visible minorities live in rural areas, small rural communities are racially and ethnically homogeneous and people who are visibly different do not always find it easy to fit in. One older person from a rural community described his interaction with a community resident who was a member of a visible minority group:

'And the druggist is a nice guy. He's Egyptian, and he's a nice guy! I told him one day, he was teasing me and I said, look if you don't be good I'm going to have to send you back, so you can plant some trees. He said there's no trees in Egypt! So I get along good with him.'

While this quote may exemplify a friendly joke, it more likely suggests that (some) rural community members reserve the right to remind people who are members of a visible minority group that they are the 'other' who must 'be good' and follow the rules established by the (white) majority in order to be tolerated. An emerging body of research examines striking invisibility in rural areas of people who are visible minorities, and suggests that partly because in rural areas these people are few and scattered, formal and informal organisations are slow to recognise and to adapt to their needs, interests and skills (Garland and Chakraborti, 2006; Commission for Rural Communities, 2007b). Exclusion also may occur because of language and other cultural barriers (Giarchi, 2006a).

Findings from our research in rural Canada showed that a higher proportion of people who are visible minorities has no effect on providing informal help to others. However, women and men in communities with higher proportions of visible minorities contributed fewer hours to volunteer activities. Men were less likely to volunteer in a wide range of organisations, while women were less likely to belong to school or neighbourhood groups and civic or community associations.

Conclusion

Rural researchers have argued that questions about how community characteristics shape the outcomes and experiences of social participation for older adults themselves must receive attention (Martinson and Minkler, 2006). We began this chapter by acknowledging this challenge. We noted that social participation has positive associations with better health and well-being. We also suggested that different community settings may influence the level of participation. Our results illustrate that certain community characteristics are associated with increased levels of social participation. Residents spent more time volunteering in communities that are less densely populated, changing in size, have a higher proportion of highly educated residents and have a higher proportion of older people. Residents helped out family and friends in more remote and less economically diverse communities with a higher proportion of highly educated and of older residents.

Can one conclude that communities with these characteristics are good places to grow old since they have higher levels of social participation? The relationship between social participation and positive outcomes may be more complex than previous acknowledged. For example, communities that are experiencing a decline in population are also losing volunteers or potential volunteers. With little potential for replacement, remaining volunteers may feel obliged to maintain or increase their contributions. The degree of need in their communities may lead some rural older adults to volunteer and to contribute more than they wish, or prevent them from freely choosing their activities. Thus it may not be the sheer volume of hours of volunteer work that leads to ageing well but whether adults have a real choice regarding meaningful activities in which to participate, whether it be volunteering or anything else (Katz, 2000; McPherson, 2004).

Even in situations where individuals feel obliged to contribute there may be positive aspects to their engagement. They may gain a sense of satisfaction and fulfilment from volunteering or helping others because they were able to improve someone else's life or make a contribution that improves their community. These opportunities also may allow them to develop new relationships or to strengthen existing relationships. When these activities are carried out under a sense of obligation these positive outcomes may not be as strong as for those who choose to contribute.

Not all community characteristics bring about higher levels of social participation; in fact, some characteristics may exclude older adults from participation. In communities where there was a higher proportion of people who are visible minorities both men and women spent less time volunteering. Also in communities with higher proportions of highly educated residents, older women spent less time volunteering. These older women are the least educated and may lack the skill sets required for the type of volunteer opportunities available in their community. Because these individuals are less likely to spend time volunteering, they are also less likely to be as connected to other members in the community. The lack of personal connections may lead to a sense of isolation and exclusion (Chapter Ten, this volume).

Volunteering is more susceptible to the influence of community characteristics than informal help to others. Higher rates of volunteering are connected to community characteristics that foster the emergence and development of volunteer organisations and opportunities (such as higher proportion of older people and highly educated people). Lower rates of volunteering are connected to community characteristics that inhibit the inclusion of residents into organisations (such as a higher proportion of people who are members of a visible minority group). However, community characteristics play only a modest role in determining the extent to which residents help one another – for example, an increase of racial and ethno-cultural diversity is not associated with decreased informal help among residents. It could mean that informal help, embedded in interpersonal relationships, is buffered from the influence of larger community contexts.

There are many factors that determine whether individuals will contribute to their community. We have illustrated that community characteristics are important in creating opportunities for social participation of adults, although sometimes characteristics of the community may also create pressures that lead to increased social participation, or make it difficult for some adults to participate. But neither social isolation nor 'coerced altruism' (McPherson, 2004) may lead to higher levels of well-being. It is important that older adults have a real choice regarding their social participation options (Tornstam, 2005) and that they have opportunities to participate in activities they like because of their own free will and preference. Having choice will make these activities rewarding and meaningful, which in turn contributes to ageing well (Katz, 2000).

NINE

Staying connected: issues of mobility of older rural adults

Bonnie Dobbs and Laurel Strain

Introduction

The increase in the number and proportion of older people, typically defined as 65 years of age and older, is one of the most profound changes affecting the industrialised, highly developed countries as well as less developed countries. In 2000, the estimated number of older people worldwide was 800 million, with a projected increase to 2 billion in 2050; 60% of those are estimated to live in rural areas (Eldar and Burger, 2000). When utilising the United Nations (UN, 2001) definition of rural as locales of fewer than 5,000 people, more than half the people in the world live in rural areas (CIESIN et al, 2005). The percentage of rural inhabitants, however, varies across countries, with greater percentages of people living in rural areas in Africa (62%) and Asia (61%), followed by Europe (32%), Oceania (26%), South America (25%) and North America (25%) (CIESIN et al, 2005).

The focus of this chapter is on the role that mobility plays in helping older rural adults stay connected within their community. Mobility refers to 'the ability of the individual to gain access through movement to the facilities that he or she desires' (Metz, 2003, p 375). It also serves as an important social connector. The quality and quantity of social interactions, feelings of isolation and loneliness, the structure of social networks and the support received from others all have been identified as predictors of health and well-being (see Cohen, 2004). Yet, while there has been a great deal of emphasis on the importance of such positive outcomes for older adults, there has been surprisingly little emphasis on the mechanisms by which older adults make their connections with people and services. Mobility, and especially driving, is a key facilitator to the integration of older rural adults into their communities.

In a seminal article, Carp (1988) conceptualised mobility as central to well-being in later life. She argued that mobility is a key determinant of the congruence or fit between life-maintenance needs such as food and clothing and the ability of older adults to live independently. Carp also hypothesised that mobility is equally important to what she called higher-order needs such as socialising, being engaged in community activities, or in worship. Carp's model is ecological, incorporating the resources and needs of older adults, as well as the social and community environments. From this perspective, 'best fit' occurs when mobility is feasible (for example, the person is able to drive) and the person is able to meet their needs independently. Personal resources such as the socioeconomic status of the person (for example, ability to afford a car), as well as community context (for example, living in a remote area) and social context (for example, access to family, friends or others who will assist with transportation) also are important. The qualities of mobility, along with these resources and contextual moderators, influence the degree of fit between needs and the individual's ability to meet those needs. Thus, within Carp's model, and indeed for many older people, mobility is the cornerstone of independence and well-being.

In this chapter, we explore the relationship between mobility in rural communities and older rural adults' abilities to meet their needs. We discuss how personal resources of older adults affect the likelihood that they will have access to transportation. Further, we consider how contextual factors might mitigate or increase the vulnerability of those at risk for unmet needs because they cannot independently meet their transportation needs. Two contexts are particularly important. Access to social networks that can assist with connections to services, to community activities and to other people can be critically important to well-being. In turn, rural community contexts such as distance from service centres and lack of public transportation often constrain the ability of older people to 'stay connected'. In Chapter Eight, Julia Rozanova et al discuss the importance of community context in enhancing participation. For these reasons, community resources, including programmes that provide alternate forms of transportation, can be key to whether older rural adults are connected to their communities.

The salience of the private vehicle

In most parts of the developed world, the car is the preferred mode of mobility. In the last two decades in the US, the use of public transportation and walking among the older population has decreased significantly (OECD, 2001) with a corresponding increase in dependency on private vehicles (Rosenbloom, 2004). Europe has also witnessed increasing reliance on private vehicles, with this reliance becoming a major trend in the post-transition economies of Eastern Europe (Scott et al, 2005).

Many older people, irrespective of rural or urban residence, are highly dependent on private vehicles (Rosenbloom, 2003). Older rural residents are more reliant on private vehicles than their urban counterparts due to the dearth of public transportation in rural areas (Turcotte, 2006) and because of geographic and environmental barriers. Thus, access to a private vehicle is a critical backdrop in the lives of older rural residents. Because of the dominance of the private vehicle as a primary means of mobility in general, and in rural areas specifically, our attention focuses on factors that affect access to a personal vehicle by older rural adults.

Access to a private vehicle can be through being a driver or a passenger. In all developed countries, possession of a driver's licence is a prerequisite for legally driving a motor vehicle. However, not all licensed drivers necessarily drive. The distinction is noteworthy. Licensing trends across age groups reveal larger discrepancies between licensing rates and driving status for older drivers than for all other age groups. Recent Canadian data indicate that a greater percentage of older Canadians are licensed to drive than those who do drive (Bess, 1999). One reason for this discrepancy may be economic marginalisation, which results in licensed drivers no longer able to afford and/or maintain a private vehicle. (See Chapter Ten, this volume, for discussions of how poverty can lead to exclusion from community resources and contacts.) Such people are more transportation-dependent than those with a driver's licence who also have access to a vehicle.

Older adults living in rural areas are more likely both to hold a driver's licence and to drive compared with those living in urban areas (Table 9.1). Sixty per cent of older persons in rural areas and small towns actively drive compared with 46% of older adults in cities with populations from 30,000 to 500,000 and higher (Bess, 1999). Differences in the rates of older drivers also exist among rural communities. In our research (Dobbs et al, 2005) in a rural county in Alberta, Canada, older residents living on farms or in hamlets with populations of 200 or fewer were more likely to drive than those who resided in villages (populations <500) or towns (populations between 1,000 and 1,800). Such differences may result from a greater need to drive among those living in communities with fewer services.

Table 9.1: Percentage of Canadians aged 65 and over who hold a driver's licence and percentage of those who are drivers, by place of residence

		Urban areas		
	Rural area[1]	Under 30,000 people	30,000 to 500,000 people	Over 500,000 people
% of people aged 65+ who hold a licence	72	62	63	52
% of people aged 65+ who are drivers	59	60	54	46

Note: [1] Defined as regions with populations fewer than 1,000 people or fewer than 400 persons per square kilometre.

Source: Bess (1999)

The potential consequences of reliance on the private vehicle as a primary means of mobility are far-reaching. Results from a number of studies support the assumption that older rural adults have more unmet needs because of transportation deficiencies in rural areas. For example, reductions in access to medical services (Arcury et al, 2005a) and to stores and services (Arcury et al, 1998) are reported for older people living in rural compared to urban areas, particularly among those who do not drive. In our research, significant percentages of older rural adults in Alberta reported unmet needs for necessary services such as shopping and banking. Significant percentages also reported not visiting their physician, dentist and/or optometrist or not having medical tests done because they did not have access to transportation.

Older adults who are dependent on others for transportation also have unmet social needs. Glasgow and Blakely (2000) noted that older rural residents who do not drive are significantly less likely to attend religious services and to be involved in community events including club activities and volunteering. Older rural non-drivers are less likely to 'get out' compared to their urban counterparts, resulting in fewer visits with friends and neighbours, reductions in participation in social activities and overall fewer contacts with their community (Bailey, 2004). In our survey of older adults in rural Alberta, the number of older people reporting unmet social needs exceeded those reporting unmet needs for goods and services or medical assistance.

Overall, access to a private vehicle, either as a driver or a passenger, plays a critical role in the lives of older rural residents, with that access acting as a significant enabler of social connectedness. Conversely, lack of transportation has the potentail to negatively affect access to services and people, resulting in unmet needs and the potential for reduction in the quality of life and increased isolation.

Personal resources and access to a private car

Given the importance of the private vehicle in rural areas for accessing goods, services and activities, it is useful to know which older rural adults are more likely to have this kind of mobility. Personal resources of older adults that have been found to be important for access to a private vehicle, either as a driver or passenger, include age, gender, marital status, socioeconomic status and health.

Age differences are clearly evident. The pattern for licensing rates and active driving status is relatively constant across age groups until age 65. From that point forward, both licensing rates and driving status decline with age. For example, 71% of Canadians aged 65-69 years are licensed to drive compared with only 23% of those 85 years of age and older (Millar, 1999). The likelihood of not going places because of lack of transportation also increases with age. Our survey of adults in rural Alberta revealed that while the lack of transportation resulted in a number of unmet needs for rural residents of all ages, it was significantly more detrimental for the older age groups. For example, compared with rural residents aged 50-64 years, residents aged 65 and older were more than twice as likely not to go to medical or dental appointments, have medical tests done, do their shopping, pick up their mail, attend church or participate in community activities because they did not have transport.

Access to private transportation also varies by gender. Similar to rates in other countries, 77% of Canadian men 65 years of age and older but only 45% of women are licensed to drive (Millar, 1999). In our Alberta survey, 87% of the older rural males drove compared with fewer than half of the older women. In fact, over half of the women compared with only one third of men reported not going places 'sometimes' or 'frequently' because of lack of transportation.

In addition, older women were less likely to go to medical appointments, shop, attend community events or socialise with friends and family than were older men because of transportation dependency.

Marital status affects access to private transportation as spouses are the most likely to be 'lift-givers' (Kostyniuk and Shope, 2003). This is particularly relevant for the current cohort of people aged 65 and over, given the differential licensing rates of older men and women. Women who are married and who have never driven or have stopped driving may be advantaged when it comes to having someone to drive them places compared with their same-age unmarried counterparts. However, because women have higher rates of widowhood, especially those in the upper age range, any advantage of the availability of a spouse tends to favour young-old women only. In addition, the lower driver licensing rate among older women negates the advantage of being married for many rural men who do not drive.

Socioeconomic status plays an important role, particularly in vehicle ownership and operation. Brown and Stommes (2004) report that poor rural households are three times less likely than non-poor rural households to have a car. For those older adults who do own vehicles, the cost of owning and operating a vehicle is higher for rural residents than for those in urban areas (Bess, 1999), placing poor older rural residents in an especially difficult position because of their greater reliance on the private vehicle. Data from a national Canadian survey indicate that people aged 65 and over with lower incomes and lower levels of education are less likely to have access to a car (Turcotte, 2006).

The health of older rural adults also needs to be taken into account, with health affecting both driving status and the need for transportation for health-related services. There is a substantial body of literature indicating that many age-related illnesses and conditions such as dementia, stroke, macular degeneration and Parkinson's disease that result in cognitive, sensory or motor impairments are associated with declines in driving ability (see Dobbs, 2005). Medically related declines in driving ability often can lead to self-imposed driving cessation or licence removal by the licensing authority. For older rural residents, this may result in lack of access to transportation during a time of greater need for that transportation. In these instances, safety concerns take precedence, but also highlight the need for transportation options in rural areas. Results from Arcury et al (2005a) illustrate the importance of a driver's licence in rural areas for accessing healthcare. In that study, adults who had a driver's licence had more than twice the healthcare visits for chronic care and almost twice the number of visits for regular check-ups than those without licences. However, compared to younger rural residents, older rural adults reported a greater need for check-ups and healthcare visits for chronic conditions (Arcury et al, 2005b), making those who are transportation-dependent most at risk for unmet healthcare needs.

In sum, older age, being female, being single and having cognitive, sensory or motor impairments put people at higher risk for dependence on others for transportation. Yet few older drivers, regardless of risk factors, consider alternatives to driving even though their life expectancy may exceed their ability to continue driving. On average, men will live approximately six years beyond the time that they have to give up driving, while for women, the time period is approximately 10 years (Foley et al, 2002). Thus, for many older rural residents, and especially for those who wish to age in place, the identification of ways to mitigate the vulnerability related to transportation dependency is critical.

Social and community contexts and access to a private vehicle

Family, friends, neighbours and communities have important roles to play in overcoming transportation deficiencies, thus enhancing the satisfaction of needs. Carp (1988) argues that strong social networks and the intergroup reliance that results from sharing rides with friends, family or neighbours strengthen levels of social integration. Such rides can reinforce an older individual's sense of being cared for and result in positive social interactions that reduce isolation and lead to the development of exchange relations that are mutually beneficial (Glasgow and Blakely, 2000). These social networks, as well as the community at large, have the potential to help older rural residents stay connected, particularly those who do not drive or those who live in communities where alternate transportation options are lacking.

Social networks

The interconnections between social networks/social capital, transportation mobility and social connectedness have been virtually ignored by both transportation researchers and scholars interested in social networks/social capital (Gray et al, 2006). Thus, despite the potential importance of kin and friends in the provision of support for older rural residents, few studies exist on the role of the social context of family, friends and neighbours in the provision of transportation-related support to them.

There are conflicting findings about the availability of a close-knit social network that may provide support to older rural adults. Internationally, the dispersion of families tends to be greater in the US, Australia and New Zealand, with three-generation households more common in the Middle East to the Pacific and in Africa (Wenger, 2001a). Adult children in Eastern and Southern Europe are more likely to live close to their parents compared with children in Northern and Western Europe. Data from a national survey of older rural Canadians (Dobbs et al, 2004) indicate the diversity of the size, composition and proximity of their social networks. In that study, only four of the 1,322 respondents (0.3%) reported having no one in their network, 8% had one to four people and the remainder reported social networks of 5–13 people. The age composition was broad, with 95% indicating that their networks consisted of people of all ages (<44, 45–64, 65+ years). Few (3%) reported having a social network consisting only of same-age peers (65+). The majority (96%) reported social networks of close kin, distant kin and non-kin, while 2% had networks of close kin only. Very few of the participants reported having social networks that lived exclusively in their community, with the majority (90%) indicating that their networks consisted of those living both nearby and at a distance.

The size, composition and proximity of social networks all are relevant to the likelihood that an older rural adult will have access to one or more people who can assist with transportation. In their chapter on changes in network composition over time, Clare Wenger and Norah Keating (Chapter Four) describe how with advanced age and increasing frailty, the ability of networks to provide needed support may be challenged. Results from the Canadian national survey (Dobbs et al, 2004) indicated that the size and age of social networks were unrelated to assistance with transportation. In addition, neither the mix of kin and non-kin nor the proximity of network members was related to assistance with transportation needs. However, fewer than 20% of these older rural adults reported the need for assistance with transportation, likely reflecting the high percentage (78%) of married respondents who had a spouse potentially able to provide transportation.

While individuals within the household are the most likely source of transportation assistance, local extended kin, friends and neighbours also may provide rides and help keep older adults connected to others. Relatives who live at a distance may also assist with scheduled medical appointments, banking or shopping that can be planned in advance. Special events such as weddings or anniversaries may be occasions for distant kin to visit and assist with such service linkages.

Overall, social networks are potential transportation resources for many older rural people. Yet, research suggests that they are reluctant to ask friends and families for rides, and do so only if the trip is essential or needed for an emergency. This reluctance to rely on friends and families, combined with the loss of autonomy in having to rely on personal networks for transportation, requires increased attention in order to better understand the challenges of providing transportation support to vulnerable rural older adults.

Community resources

At the community level, transportation service provision in rural areas often is fragmented or unavailable. Older adults are particularly vulnerable to lack of public transportation (Herold et al, 2002), most likely due to a combination of fewer personal resources such as health and income and the greater likelihood that they do not drive. Notably, older people frequently rate the transportation options in their communities, such as public transportation, taxis and shuttle services, as poor (Dobbs et al, 2004). A primary challenge for rural communities is to develop, implement and sustain older people-friendly alternative transportation systems with limited resources and in contexts that may include low population density and long distances to service centres.

An example of a comprehensive approach to transportation for older adults is the Supplemental Transportation Programs for Seniors (STPs) project, initiated in the US in 2000, with programmes in urban, suburban and rural areas (Beverly Foundation and AAA Foundation for Traffic Safety, 2004). The programmes developed under this initiative are community-based and designed to enable older people to 'get where they need to go'. The majority of the rural programmes are non-profit, with funding primarily from grants and rider fees. Compared with the urban/suburban programmes, rural STPs provide more transportation for medical purposes to address problems of distance from acute and specialist medical services. They are more likely to use paid drivers than volunteer drivers in recognition of the limited voluntary capacity in small communities, and to deliver door-to-door service. Finally, rural programmes are less likely to charge user fees in an attempt to make the service accessible to those on limited incomes.

STPs are a good example of community-based transportation programmes that contribute to rural communities being 'older people-friendly' (see Chapter Eleven for a critical review of elements of age-friendly communities). These characteristics are:

- *availability:* transportation exists and is available when needed (for example, transportation is at hand evenings and/or weekends);
- *accessibility:* transportation can be reached and used (for example, bus stairs can be negotiated; bus seats are high enough; van comes to the door);
- *acceptability:* deals with standards relating to conditions such as cleanliness (for example, the vehicle is not dirty); safety (for example, bus stops are located in safe areas); and user-friendliness (for example, drivers/operators are courteous and helpful);
- *affordability:* deals with costs (for example, fees are affordable; fees are comparable with or less than driving a car; vouchers or coupons help defray out-of-pocket expenses);
- *adaptability:* transportation can be modified or adjusted to meet special needs (for example, wheelchair can be accommodated; trip chaining is possible).

An important consideration in developing, implementing and sustaining transportation options for older rural adults is the nature of the community and its residents. Because of the diversity in their support networks and their communities, a 'one size fits all' approach to transportation issues faced by rural older adults is unlikely to be successful. Rather, community-based transportation programmes that address the needs of older people in their community by allowing them to go where and when they need to go in a manner that is acceptable, affordable and adaptable to their needs are those that are most likely to be successful.

Conclusion

Issues related to mobility and independence for older people in rural areas are of great concern now and will continue to be in upcoming decades. The private vehicle plays a pivotal role in meeting the transportation needs of rural older people. However, contextual factors such as age, gender, marital status, socioeconomic status and health can affect access to a private vehicle. The heterogeneity among the older population is such that some older rural residents will continue to meet their needs, either through driving or through reliance on their social networks or community-based transportation services. At the same time, there are vulnerable rural older people who are likely to have unmet basic and social needs due to self- or externally imposed driving cessation, diminished social networks and/or limited or absent community-based transportation. Those who are most at risk for unmet needs are rural older people who are older, female, single/widowed, of lower socioeconomic status and/or in poor health.

Social networks play an important role in helping rural older people meet their transportation needs. However, not all rural older people are embedded in supportive social networks. Community-based transportation programmes are important sources of transportation but those programmes often are absent or fragmented in rural areas.

Overall, as argued by Carp (1988), mobility plays a central role in the promotion of independence and well-being of older rural adults, in that it is one of the primary means for meeting both life-maintenance and higher-order needs. However, the heterogeneity of both the older age group and rural communities is increasingly recognised. Given the prominent role that mobility plays in the health and well-being of rural older people, greater attention to senior transportation issues that recognises the diversity among older adults and among rural communities is needed if there are to be improvements in mobility for vulnerable older people in rural areas. In addition, personal resources, the community context and the social context all need to be taken into consideration in an examination of this complex issue.

TEN

Ageing and social exclusion in rural communities

Thomas Scharf and Bernadette Bartlam

Introduction

In this chapter, we adopt the concept of social exclusion as a means to explore issues around disadvantage faced by older people in rural communities. The focus on social exclusion is important in casting light on the varied, and often hidden, nature of disadvantage experienced by older rural residents in many Western societies. Such disadvantage potentially challenges views about the degree to which rural communities represent good places in which to grow old. Our approach is underpinned by a critical gerontology perspective. With its focus on the structural causes of inequalities in later life, its appreciation of the cumulative impacts of disadvantages faced by different groups of older people and its value-based commitment to bringing the voices of older people to the fore (Bernard and Phillips, 2000; Holstein and Minkler, 2007), the critical perspective lends itself especially well to the analysis of social exclusion among older people in rural settings. Drawing on findings from a qualitative study, we examine individuals' accounts of exclusion, explore lifecourse influences on exclusion and assess the impacts of exclusion on quality of life. The chapter concludes by highlighting the distinctive features of rural older people's social exclusion, and suggesting some ways in which rural policy might serve to reduce such exclusion.

Rural perspectives on social exclusion and ageing

Current research and policy debates in Western societies around social exclusion provide an ideal framework for exploring the situation of rural older people. While such debates primarily focus on the situation of children, young people and families, a growing body of research explores ways in which older people experience forms of exclusion (Scharf et al, 2005b; Patsios, 2006). Defined as 'the dynamic process of being shut out, fully or partially, from any of the social, economic, political and cultural systems which determine the social integration of a person in society' (Walker and Walker, 1997, p 8), the multidimensional nature of exclusion is reflected in attempts to operationalise the concept in empirical studies (Burchardt et al, 2002; Pantazis et al, 2006). While there are significant overlaps between the concepts of social exclusion and poverty, with Bauman (1998, p 37) arguing that 'poverty means being excluded from whatever passes for a "normal life"', exclusion discourse extends the traditionally more limited view of poverty as representing the lack of material resources. Alongside a focus on poverty, measures of exclusion typically incorporate such dimensions as individuals' (lack of) engagement in meaningful social relationships, (lack of) participation in civic activities and (lack of) access to formal services (Pantazis et al, 2006). Reflecting the importance of the immediate living environment to individuals' well-being, other approaches incorporate a 'neighbourhood' or 'community' dimension of exclusion (Scharf et al, 2005b).

Although primarily discussed in an urban context, the concept of social exclusion is also relevant in rural studies (Philip and Shucksmith, 2003; Commins, 2004). Nevertheless, research and policy evidence relating to exclusion and disadvantage of rural older people is limited (Shucksmith, 2003; Giarchi, 2006a), thereby contributing to the perpetuation of a range of stereotypes concerning rural ageing (Wenger, 2001b; Lowe and Stephenson, 2002). Among such myths are those that highlight the integration of rural older people within close and supportive family networks; draw attention to the supportive nature of rural communities; and suggest that rural older people have fewer service needs because they are healthier and more satisfied with life than their urban counterparts (Wenger, 2001b).

One reason why such stereotypes persist is that rural older people's social exclusion may not be easily recognisable. Equally, there is a tendency in research and policy to homogenise rural communities, with the result that the often pronounced physical differences between contrasting types of rural community are ignored. For example, the UK Department for Work and Pensions' strategy document *Opportunity age* (DWP, 2005) highlights the difficulty of assessing the material disadvantage of rural older people:

> Because deprivation is not often found in concentrated clusters of people, it is harder to identify – and therefore harder to tackle. Older people in rural areas may be suffering from acute deprivation, but may remain hidden from view among apparent neighbouring affluence. (DWP, 2005, p 62)

Similar findings are reported in Ireland (Commins, 2004) and the US (Milbourne, 2004). Since most older people in rural areas report good physical and mental health, and visit a general practitioner less often than those in urban areas (Countryside Agency, 2003), there is a popular perception that rural older people are a relatively advantaged social group. However, evidence from a range of countries suggests that rural older people experience worse health and socioeconomic outcomes than the general older population (Rowles and Johansson, 1993; ACSA and NRHA, 2004). This view may be reinforced by disparities between apparently objective assessments of disadvantage and rural older people's own subjective accounts. Consequently, older people living in low-income households may seek to qualify their experience of poverty by emphasising more positive aspects of rural life (Philip and Shucksmith, 2003). This in turn reflects a prevalent attitude among rural older people – willingly taken up by service providers – that emphasises notions of self-sufficiency, independence and pride (Wenger, 2001b; Bevan and Croucher, 2006). This attitude of self-sufficiency is evident in Chapter Eleven (this volume) in which Jacquie Eales et al describe 'stoic' older people who forego needed services if they are not readily available because they do not want to bother others with requests for assistance.

Notwithstanding a limited empirical base, it is nevertheless possible to summarise existing evidence concerning disadvantage among rural older people in relation to at least three key dimensions of exclusion. First, *exclusion from material resources* – reflecting the fundamental importance of adequate income and material conditions in underpinning well-being in later life – is evident in data on low incomes. North American and Australasian studies show rural residence to be associated with lower income and higher poverty than the average (Glasgow, 1993; Vartanian and McNamara, 2002, p 533; ACSA/NRHA, 2004; McCracken et al, 2005). In 2000/01, one quarter of UK pensioners in rural districts were living on low incomes (Countryside Agency, 2002, p 75) and those in remote rural areas are the most likely to live on low incomes (Gilbert et al, 2006). Poverty for some rural older people may be compounded by the non-take-up of state benefits, with UK research suggesting that take-up rates of key benefits are lower in rural than urban areas (NAO, 2002, p 26).

Second, *exclusion from social relations* identifies older people who are socially isolated, lonely or unable to participate in socially valued activities as liable to reduced well-being. Studies from Western nations highlight the potential for rural older people to be excluded from social relations, as reflected in research on social isolation (Findlay and Cartwright, 2002; Bevan and Croucher, 2006) and social networks (Wenger, 1997; Dobbs et al, 2004). Estimates of the prevalence of isolation among older people vary – often as a result of differences in measurement approaches (Cattan, 2002). However, isolation appears to be most pronounced among those who live alone, who are without local family and who lack adequate material resources (Le Mesurier, 2003). Clare Wenger and Norah Keating (Chapter Four, this volume) illustrate how this isolation from others becomes increasingly problematic as people reach very old age and need assistance.

Third, *exclusion from services* reflects the importance of basic services in and beyond the home as people age, and especially when individuals have health and social care needs (Bevan and Croucher, 2006). Access to services varies considerably across Western nations. In the UK, 40% of older people in rural areas report difficulty in accessing services (Countryside Agency, 2003). In Canada, around 30% of rural older people live in communities that lack a physician or a pharmacy (Dobbs et al, 2004) and, in its most remote areas, the provision of homecare nursing is perceived to be 'almost impossible' (McCracken et al, 2005). In New Zealand, limited access to healthcare practitioners has been linked to longer hospital stays for rural older people (Koopman-Boyden et al, 2006). In terms of formal service support, rural older people in the UK are less likely to receive help from social services to live at home than those living in urban areas (Countryside Agency/Age Concern, 2005). Restricted mobility and lack of access to transport are regarded as key problems for older people wherever they live. However, in rural areas the greater distance between people's homes and basic services may exacerbate such disadvantage (Giarchi, 2006a). As a result, access to a car is often the difference between receiving or not receiving services. While 77% of women and 94% of men aged 65 and over in rural areas of Canada still drive (Dobbs et al, 2004), 40% of people aged 75 and over in rural areas of the UK lack access to a car (DEFRA, 2004, p 68).

Data relating to other forms of exclusion in rural communities are lacking, most notably in respect of participation in civic activities and community integration. Two chapters in this book begin to address these gaps. In Chapter Seven, Janet Fast and Jenny de Jong Gierveld document participation in civic activities such as volunteering; in Chapter Eight, Julia Rozanova et al describe how community features such as remoteness influence such engagement. Existing research does highlight the diverse ways in which rural older people might experience disadvantage. While exclusion does not represent the norm, there are important gaps in the rural evidence base. The critical gerontology approach argues that the voices of those who experience such disadvantages should be heard more clearly, especially if decision-making processes affecting their lives are to be influenced (Holstein and Minkler, 2007). However, few accounts exist of disadvantage from the perspectives of those who live on a low income, experience social isolation, have limited access to services or find it difficult to cope with changes in their communities.

In the remaining sections of this chapter, we therefore draw on a qualitative study involving in-depth interviews with rural older people in order to go some way towards addressing this knowledge gap. The study built on the methodological approach adopted in earlier research on disadvantage among older people living in urban areas, and occurred in three linked phases (Scharf and Bartlam, 2006a). First, we identified key stakeholder groups already working with potentially excluded older people in three English counties. By engaging with contrasting community-based groups – a welfare advice organisation, a community transport scheme, a branch of an older people's charity, a rural carers' outreach scheme and a branch of a mental health charity – we sought to capture the diversity of exclusion faced by rural older people. Second, we developed a short screening questionnaire to identify people aged 60 and over who were experiencing one or more forms of exclusion. The tool was administered by staff and volunteers from the stakeholder groups, and 91 questionnaires were completed. Reflecting individuals' responses to particular questions, participants were assessed on the basis of their vulnerability to four forms of exclusion: exclusion from material resources, social relations, services and the 'community'. Twenty-one in-depth interviews were subsequently undertaken with older people identified as experiencing at least one form of exclusion. The third phase of the research involved data analysis.

Interviews were transcribed and subject to content analysis, with a focus on generating information that would give voice to individuals' accounts of different types of exclusion.

Exclusion in rural communities: older people's voices

In summarising findings from the empirical study, our analysis is organised according to the four domains of exclusion under investigation, with selected quotes from in-depth interviews used to illustrate aspects of disadvantage experienced by rural older people.

Exclusion from material resources

While several research participants claimed not to be unduly affected by limited material resources, most narratives revealed at least some difficulty in getting by financially. For some, there was evidence of real financial hardship, with money worries having a profoundly negative impact on well-being. One male participant, for example, described having a mental health breakdown following the bankruptcy of his farm business. A 74-year-old widow conveyed a sense of profound worry over her finances: "sometimes I find it very difficult. Same as just at the moment now, I've had a lot of bills to pay and it's really getting me run down, you see". Elsewhere, relatively small items of expenditure were felt to be beyond reach. One 79-year-old woman found it difficult to afford to participate in meetings of the Women's Institute (WI): "Well, WI is, yes, very, very expensive, because you pay 30p when you go in. And think, that's for your cup of tea and cake and then there's a raffle, so you reckon it up in the year…".

Even though several participants had acquired housing assets, either through inheritance or by paying off a mortgage, this capital was tied up in their homes and did not allow for more than a modest standard of living. Many participants described managing their finances with great care, seeking to avoid seemingly unnecessary expenses or incurring debt. A 60-year-old divorced man typified the prevailing approach: "As long as you're thrifty and you don't spend on excessive things it's a reasonable standard of living". A 74-year-old man, who was the main carer of his wife, was finding life difficult, but was reluctant to borrow money to pay for the upkeep of the family home: "I mean there's no way we're borrowing. I mean if we've got bills coming in, we just save…. When you get to our age you've got more or less everything that you want".

Emphasising the apparent capacity of rural households to manage through difficult financial times, a female participant described a very modest lifestyle. She referred back to the time when she and her husband were tenant farmers, arguing that a key indicator of their ability to manage was simply having enough to eat: "We'd always had pretty well of food. Being up at the farm we'd have something killed and we'd have plenty to eat, either pork or chicken…". Reflecting modest expectations in relation to their finances, participants prioritised expenditure on food and household bills. Even where finances were stretched, most sought to manage without applying for welfare support. Former farmers appeared especially unwilling to seek financial help:

> 'I mean actually you live in a cocooned little world when you're farming or living in the rural areas. You don't know anything about housing benefits, you don't know anything about Disability Living Allowance ... you're so wrapped up in surviving and work. Well, I never stopped work. I just totally burnt myself out. And that's what happens with farmers, they will not ask for help, they're too proud, and I was too proud and I thought the only way they're going to get me off the farm is in a pine box. Well, looking at it now it seems a totally ridiculous attitude.'

Where participants had overcome an initial reluctance to claim benefits and support from the state, this was usually the result of a financial crisis or a sudden deterioration in a family member's state of health. Other participants managed without state support because they were able to call on income from alternative sources. Family members, friends and neighbours occasionally appeared willing to contribute to household finances – either directly, as in the case of one female participant whose son-in-law helped out with food shopping, or indirectly, by offering lifts or helping to manage a bank account.

Exclusion from material resources was usually linked to low incomes during individuals' working lives. People who have limited access to the labour market or who have spent their adult lives in low-paid (agricultural) employment are unlikely to have sufficient money set aside to provide for a comfortable retirement:

> 'I started working there when I left school, seven in the morning till seven at night for 15 shillings a week. And I left there when mother had her stroke and the wage was £4 a week. After her'd died, I got a job in the kitchen up at school and that was the most was £24 a week. For 14 weeks' holiday a year you only got a retainer, which was £13. In 1980 I'd lost my hours from 30 down to 15 because children stopped having hot dinners.... Consequently I've never handled a big wage. So consequently, you know, you come home, you'd be upset, you'd have a cry, how am I going to manage? Well then, what I did, I thought I could do a bit of babysitting, and that is what I did....'

While most participants reported having a good quality of life, this tended to reflect attitudes generated over the lifecourse, and individuals' (often limited) expectations. Nevertheless, few participants had expectations of a higher standard of living, and there was a pervasive belief that it was the individual's responsibility to make the best out of a difficult financial situation. This was exemplified by a couple who had coped with the strain of bankruptcy and an enforced move away from their farm, and simply felt that they "couldn't be any better off" under their present circumstances.

Exclusion from social relations

Exclusion from social relations was explored in relation to the themes of isolation and loneliness. For some participants, living in a rural community was synonymous with isolation, with one participant simply stating: "it's a lonely experience in a small village". An 82-year-old widow reported finding the winter months to be a particularly difficult time: "The clocks alter, you draw the curtains at four o'clockish and you don't see anybody again. And I'm off the main road, so I can't even see people going past". While some participants saw compensating factors in rural life and described issues around independence, privacy and freedom as key to their determination to 'age in place', others saw few redeeming features. One woman in particular had moved into a small retirement development about a mile outside a large village on the death of her husband. At the time of interview, she was the main carer for her wheelchair-bound, 93-year-old mother and reported often feeling lonely and having a very poor quality of life. Unable to drive due to poor vision, she found living in the countryside incredibly isolating:

> 'I like people. I'm a person who needs people. So some days unless the 'phone goes, I don't speak to anybody. So if I was in the town I could then push mum into the town and we could talk to people, or if mum wasn't with me anymore I could just walk round the shops and meet people.'

The fact that rural communities had changed during the course of participants' lives appeared to reinforce some people's isolation. This often arose when participants' health was poor or when they had little in common with younger in-migrants, as in the case of an 86-year-old widow:

> 'Well, the few [local residents] just around are friendly, but you don't see anything much now of what I call the new people up in the barns and that. They're very nice when you do see them, but they've sort of divided the village in half almost now. Because they're at the top and we're at the bottom, we don't mix very much.'

Alongside such experiences of exclusion, several participants reported the existence of a strong sense of community and of supportive relationships with family, friends and neighbours. Where care and support were provided, this came mainly from family members. The importance of such support was illustrated by a 78-year-old woman who lived with her husband on an isolated smallholding. The participant had health problems, although her mobility was good. However, she had never learnt to drive a car, and her husband, who had become extremely frail, could no longer do so. At the time of interview, the couple were receiving a considerable degree of help from friends and family:

> 'Our son-in-law comes over most days, doesn't he, to look at the horses and to muck out. Rachel – that's our daughter – she will pop in … in the evening as she did last night because she did all my shopping. Now on Thursdays, usually a friend of ours comes and takes me to [local town] to do shopping in Sainsbury's and just potter … and two very good friends come usually once a week because Peter, the husband, cuts the lawns for us. Gladys sometimes helps him, his wife, but they're in their sixties and not young, and then Gladys will come in and chat, and have a cup of tea or whatever….'

For many participants, good or poor quality of life was closely related to the quality of personal relationships. For example, one woman felt that she had a good quality of life, and commented that "having people that care" was the most important thing. By contrast, another woman perceived her quality of life to be very poor, and expressed a desire to relocate from her present village into a town. However, she recognised that it would be difficult to put her 93-year-old mother through the associated upheaval. As a result, she felt trapped in her home and, when asked about what makes her life good, simply replied: "Being alive, that's all I can say. And some days I'm not bothered one way or the other".

Such a culture of caring for family members, and of providing support to vulnerable members of the local community, was evident in several narratives. A preference for family care was often bound up in a desire to maintain a rural way of life, and to avoid becoming dependent on the state: "… it put the fear of the Lord into them [my parents], the thought of them having to go into old folks' homes after they'd been used to seeing the sun get up and dead silence". In some cases, especially where people had aged in place, longstanding neighbours also appeared willing to provide help and support. One male participant, who was caring for his disabled wife, reported having an excellent relationship with a (younger) neighbour, who had told him: "if you want me any hour of the day or night, two, three, four o'clock in the morning, I will leap over the wall".

In terms of individuals' lifecourses, pathways into social isolation and loneliness occasionally represented a longstanding condition linked to the difficulty of coping with the loss of a partner and/or child earlier in life. In other instances, exclusion reflected the impact of losses, combined with the onset of chronic health problems, which had occurred later in life. Such losses tended to coincide with the difficulty of forming relationships with new neighbours in a rapidly changing rural community. While widowhood represented an important transition point in the lives of many female participants, for men the equivalent transition was relationship breakdown and subsequent divorce. Moreover, several participants, both male and female, perceived the transition to a caring role as a difficult and isolating experience.

Exclusion from services

Two key issues emerged in relation to service issues: loss of formal services from rural communities and difficulties of reaching services located further afield. Loss of services diminished some participants' quality of life and ability to engage in social activities:

> '… years ago we used to have a little village hut and then, when they built the new hut at [larger village one-and-a-half miles away], what they call the parish hall, they said this [one] wasn't good enough to have functions in, you know, and it was sold, it went. But it was very good and then of course everybody went then because there was no transport. But we had lovely times in there, much happier than in the parish hall, I think. But of course, the people's changed and the building's changed.'

At a more fundamental level, the absence of street lighting and footpaths left several participants – especially those with reduced mobility – unable to walk around their communities. One woman, who was caring for her profoundly physically and mentally disabled mother, was effectively trapped indoors by the lack of a proper footpath.

Most participants identified transport as being a key concern when it came to accessing more distant services, and all participants regarded physical access to resources and amenities as being dependent on health and mobility. Even if there was a good public bus service, poor health meant that the service could not be used. The independence and mobility afforded by having a car was explained clearly by one woman who expressed difficulty in walking: "Just to go round to the village hall, which is just around the corner, we have to go in the car. The only problem would be if we couldn't drive any more, then we would have to leave it [the hamlet]".

Exclusion from the 'community'

The issue of area change was one of the contrasts between rural communities that were perceived to be growing – as evidenced by the construction of new housing and a rising population – and those that were stagnating. Many research participants had lived in their current settlement for a considerable length of time, and a number had spent their entire lives not just in the same location but also in the same house. All could comment on features of their communities that they liked – the attractive surroundings, local family, friends and neighbours, the peace and quiet – and most were very satisfied with their community as a place in which to age. However, some were concerned about recent changes, and many participants commented on the impact of population change on the quality of social life. The view of a more positive past was frequently contrasted with an apparent loss of intimacy in current times:

> 'All doors open, you could go anywhere. You set off from here, I was reared near up there so we used to go and demand a cup of tea. Graeme lived down there, so we used to stroll in there; Bob Saunders lived there, you could stroll in there; another uncle lived there. It was the same all through the village. It was wherever you went, "are you coming in here and having a cuppa?". You know what I mean? Oh, it was much nicer. When we were kids, we'd got nothing, but I wouldn't swap it for today.'

Population change also meant that many younger community residents now led busy work lives that took them away from their homes during the day. This too affected the quality of people's social interactions:

> '... the young ones that are coming in ... they all go to work. They go out in a morning, eight o'clock to half-past and then, after I walk up to the bus there's nobody to say hello to, you know. The whole set-up has altered and is still altering ... and it's not the same any more.'

While some participants noted that new housing developments also had certain advantages, in particular by sustaining the presence of key services, such as a doctor's surgery, a chemist or a local shop, such developments also had their downsides. A central source of concern for some older people was the lack of affordability of homes for younger family members. This meant that children were unable to live close to, and provide more support to, ageing parents.

Conclusion

The empirical study emphasises the diverse ways in which rural older people might experience exclusion, challenging assumptions about the idyllic nature of rural ageing and the degree to which rural communities represent good places in which to grow old. Our data show how limited material resources, poor-quality social relationships, lack of access to services and changes within rural communities can interact to reduce well-being. Evidence was also found of the impact of lifecourse factors and life events in generating exclusion in later life. Three key features emphasise the distinctiveness of rural older people's exclusion.

First, our study highlights the dispersed, and often hidden, nature of disadvantage in rural locations. While exclusion in urban areas tends to become concentrated in particular (deprived) neighbourhoods, in rural areas it is likely to be spread unevenly – and often unpredictably – across hamlets, villages and small towns. Our study also reflected the diversity of those experiencing exclusion in rural communities, with disadvantage faced by older men and women, by people from a range of socioeconomic backgrounds, by those with both good and poor health and by people living alone and those sharing their households with others.

Second, in bringing the voices of excluded older people in rural areas to the fore, we were struck by the tendency of those affected to downplay and internalise their experience of disadvantage. However, despite their disadvantage, most participants reported a good quality of life. These factors contribute further to the camouflaging of rural social exclusion. Indeed, the ways in which rural older people talk so indirectly about their exclusion is noteworthy. This was especially evident in participants' accounts of their material circumstances, but also applied to other forms of disadvantage. While most participants in the empirical study identified themselves as getting by reasonably well financially, the interviews provided evidence of real hardship. One reason why many participants were able to report a good quality of life was the provision of a substantial degree of support by family, friends and neighbours. This was evident in relation to at least three of the forms of exclusion. In terms of material disadvantage, family members could be called on to provide direct financial help or to assist in the process of claiming state benefits. The contribution of family, friends and neighbours in overcoming isolation and loneliness was a recurring feature of many narratives. Access to services within the local area and further away was often facilitated by the willingness of members of older people's informal support networks to provide help with transportation.

Third, the physical isolation of some rural settlements, and the socially isolating impact of changes within local populations appeared to exclude some older people from their communities. Many rural areas in Western nations have experienced a considerable growth in population in recent decades as a result of the in-migration of relatively affluent people from urban areas. For some people taking part in our study, especially those ageing in place, such population change has fundamentally altered the character of their community, and generated feelings of dissatisfaction. Many participants commented on the difficulty of forming and maintaining close relationships with recent in-migrants. Such issues seem to threaten fundamental personal assumptions about both individual identity and collective identity as a village community, and indeed what it means to be a rural older person.

Drawing on the distinctive characteristics of rural social exclusion, we would like to conclude with some comments on ways in which public policy might contribute to making rural communities better places in which to grow old. First, we would argue that while current policy making in nations such as the UK is correct to focus on disadvantage linked to some rural older people's social isolation and lack of access to services, this should also be matched by greater awareness of the impact of material disadvantage on older people's daily lives. The dispersed and hidden nature of rural poverty suggests that outreach work, which seeks to overcome attitudinal barriers to benefit take-up and to maximise rural older people's incomes, is likely to become increasingly important within the context of an ageing rural older population.

Second, our study emphasised that rural communities may not be such pleasant places in which to age for people who lack transport or who have reduced mobility. The sense of being confined to one's place of residence was especially pronounced in some rural settlements, where the absence or poor maintenance of footpaths, the lack of street lighting, and fast-moving traffic were reported. It is, therefore, important for rural policy to consider the needs of older people when planning transport services. In some countries, further public support for innovative forms of service provision, such as community buses, taxis or Dial-a-Ride schemes, could represent an appropriate way of promoting rural older people's social inclusion. Bonnie Dobbs and Laurel Strain (Chapter Nine) also describe interventions to support mobility of older rural adults.

Finally, there is the issue of community change. In the study reported here, many participants reflected on the apparent deterioration in the quality of social relationships as a result of population change, and suggested that rising housing costs were making it increasingly difficult for family members to live in close proximity to one another. In our view, policies designed to improve the affordability of housing in rural areas would represent a step in the right direction when it comes to addressing the support needs of longstanding residents of some rural communities. Nevertheless, the maintenance and development of appropriate health and social care services to meet the needs of older people and their carers who lack proximate family support will continue to be an important theme for rural policy makers. Addressing these policy challenges is by no means straightforward, as shown by Joanie Sims-Gould and Anne Martin-Matthews (Chapter Five) in relation to provision of rural homecare. However, by reducing social exclusion, rural communities can become much better places in which to grow old.

ELEVEN

Age-friendly rural communities

Jacquie Eales, Janice Keefe and Norah Keating

Introduction

Much concern has been expressed about the demographic changes that are the hallmark of population ageing. Projections of rapidly increasing numbers of older adults have led to a great deal of discussion in policy and practice communities about the kinds of services and support that they might require. At times, the discussion has taken on the tone of 'apocalyptic demography' (Gee, 2000, p 5) with older adults seen as a drain on public programmes and service infrastructure. In this context, rural areas have been viewed with apprehension since their populations are ageing more quickly than those in cities (Wagner, 2006).

Recently, there has been a shift in the discourse about population ageing away from problematising ageing towards an interest in creating settings in which older adults can flourish. The United Nations emphasises supportive environments in its International Plan of Action on Ageing: neighbourhoods and communities that 'enable elderly people to continue to live, if they so wish, in locations that are familiar to them, where their involvement in the community may be longstanding and where they will have the opportunity to lead a rich, normal, and secure life' (UN, 2003, p 12). There is increased interest in communities as providers of these supportive environments, and in how community settings create contexts in which older adults are able to flourish (Wahl and Weisman, 2003; Bronstein et al, 2006). International organisations have begun to articulate the ways in which communities might enhance the lives of older adults. The World Health Organization (WHO) (2006) has coined the term 'age-friendly' as a descriptor of such communities. Age-friendly communities are described as having policies, services and structures related to the natural, human-built and social environments that enable older people to 'live in security, enjoy good health and continue to participate fully in society' (WHO, 2006, p 1). WHO describes the main elements of age-friendly communities as the recognition of diversity among older adults, promotion of inclusion and contribution, respect for decisions and lifestyle choices and responsiveness to age-related needs and preferences.

In July 2006, WHO initiated the Global Age-Friendly Cities project to encourage countries across the world to enhance the environmental and social factors that contribute to healthy ageing in their cities. Concerns have also been expressed about rural areas where older adults may have access to lower levels of these resources (Bronstein et al, 2006; WHO, 2006). For example, Joseph and Cloutier-Fisher (2005) reported that many rural communities in New Zealand and Canada have lost both private and public sector services. Keefe et al (2004) note that rural communities may differ considerably in the amount of social support available to older adults. In fact, there are persistent and often contradictory assumptions about the experience of ageing in rural places. Speaking from a UK perspective, Scharf et al (2005c, p 186) note that:

> Alongside the image of an older person deeply embedded within a supportive social network, there is also the image of the rural older person who has been abandoned by his or her family and is dependent upon a poorly developed service infrastructure in order to get by in life.

Canada has taken up the challenge of addressing these assumptions by launching an initiative focused specifically on identifying the characteristics of age-friendly rural and remote communities (Government of Manitoba, 2007).

The 'resources' approach to understanding age-friendly communities

One approach to understanding these assumptions about the lives of older adults in rural places is to describe features of communities that are considered to be age-friendly. A generation ago, Lawton (1977) already was speaking to the issue of community resources. He said that:

> The most salient single aspect of the older person's living environment ... is the resources available to him within accessible distance, whether they be life sustaining facilities such as shops, medical care and police protection, or life enriching facilities, such as family, friends, cultural opportunities or a senior centre. (Lawton, 1977, p 277)

Many of these features are examples of elements of natural, human-built and social environments. Drawing on the literature on factors that contribute to age-friendly urban communities (Billig, 2004; Bronstein et al, 2006; Masotti et al, 2006; WHO, 2006) and the environmental determinants of ageing well (Kahana et al, 2003), Box 11.1 summarises elements of age-friendly communities within each of these three environments.

The natural environment comprises the physical and biological elements of nature, such as air, climate and water, elements that provide the essential resource base for life (Bubolz and Sontag, 1993). Clean well water, adequate waste removal systems and clean air are key health determinants for all rural citizens, and especially for older people who may have weaker immunity to diseases and infections (Short, 2006). Some older adults may retire from the city to the countryside in search

Box 11.1: Age-friendly communities: the resources approach

Natural environment

- good air/water quality
- climate and topography

Human-built environment

- appropriate, accessible, affordable housing
- accessible stores and services
- barrier-free and enabling interior and exterior spaces
- accessible public and private transportation

Social environment

- opportunities to maintain relationships with family members and friends
- inclusive opportunities for civic, cultural, educational and voluntary engagement
- activities, programmes and information to promote health, social and spiritual well-being.

of the 'good life' (Rowles, 1998, p 113), clear of such elements that make cities undesirable. Attractive features of the natural environment may draw older adults to rural communities and provide opportunities for participation and enjoyment. Indeed, Bennett (1996) found that beauty, tranquillity and opportunities for outdoor recreation such as golf and fishing were incentives for many people to retire to rural communities on the East Coast of the US.

The human-built environment refers to the alterations and transformations people make to the natural physical-biological environment for survival, sustenance and the attainment of other ends (Bubolz and Sontag, 1993). Human-built resources include housing, roads, stores and services. Residential homes provide a sense of constancy and predictability in the lives of older adults (Wahl and Weisman, 2003) and appropriate and accessible housing is seen as an important element of age-friendly communities. Having homes as well as communities that are barrier-free fosters the mobility and independence of older adults, particularly those with disabilities. In Sweden, many older people stated that uneven paving stones, icy streets and steps at entrances hindered their ability to access and use public facilities (Valdemarsson et al, 2005). Retail stores and services such as post offices, grocery stores, banks, physicians and pharmacies contribute to the maintenance of older adults' day-to-day lives, while some community support services are targeted primarily at those who are frail (Billig, 2004). The retrenchment of services in some rural areas may detract from these communities' abilities to support such older adults. Although public or private transportation is important to accessing stores and services, the dearth of accessible transportation in rural areas is longstanding (Gray et al, 2006).

The social environment comprises other people, social and economic institutions such as community organisations and events, and cultural constructions such as language and cultural norms (Bubolz and Sontag, 1993). Social opportunities, such as civic, cultural and voluntary engagement, are viewed as important aspects of age-friendly communities because ageing is meant to be 'active'. Opportunities for activity among older adults in turn are perceived as contributing to successful ageing (Katz, 2000; Billig, 2004; Masotti et al, 2006). Yet others argue that the over-promotion of civic engagement and active later years potentially devalues frail older people, those with disabilities or those whose economic situations prevent them from remaining active (Martinson and Minkler, 2006). Similarly, social support from family and friends is also viewed as an important element of age-friendly communities (WHO, 2006). Yet older adults may differ in their desire for social connections. In rural England some older adults are well connected to other people and value their social connections, while others prefer less connection, placing higher value on their privacy (Manthorpe et al, 2004).

The identification of resources that derive from the natural, human-built and social environments is an important first step in conceptualising age-friendly communities because it provides a contextual view of older adults. This approach highlights communities as places in which older adults interact and are interdependent with their living environments, including the natural, human-built and social contexts in which they live (Wahl and Weisman, 2003). However, the salience of these environments may differ among older adults (Kahana et al, 2003) and influence their experiences of the age-friendliness of their community. Some older adults are active, while others are not. Some older adults value their social connections with people, while others are more private. Rural communities are also diverse. Some are service rich, while others are service poor. Some are able to maintain well their infrastructure such as roads, pavements and building access, while others may struggle. In expanding our conceptualisation of age-friendly rural communities, it is essential to consider the diversity among both older adults and rural communities, and the interdependent relationship between people and their environments.

The 'best-fit' approach to understanding age-friendly communities

In their statement of what constitutes an age-friendly community, WHO emphasises the importance of recognising diversity among older adults in their preferences, needs, resources and lifestyle choices (WHO, 2006). Yet the resource approach to determining what might constitute an age-friendly community does not explicitly take into account these systematic differences.

There is a need to expand our conceptualisation of age-friendly communities to reflect an acknowledgement of diversity among older adults. The concept of 'best fit' is used as the basis for this expanded conceptualisation. The idea is that one can only understand the relevance of community characteristics by understanding how well particular resources meet the needs of different groups of older adults. For example, accessible stores and services may be particularly important to older adults with physical disabilities or mobility limitations but less relevant to those who have the financial and health resources to shop anywhere.

From this perspective, age-friendly communities provide the best fit between the preferences and needs of older adults and the resources of the community in which they live (Kahana et al, 2003).

Recent research on older adults living in rural communities in Canada has given us some insight into the ways in which older adults interact differently with the natural, human-built and social environments. In the remainder of this chapter, the salience of these rural community resources is compared with the preferences, needs and lifestyle choices of two different groups of older adults (Eales et al, 2006). The first group is community active older adults who epitomise the image of active ageing and 'busy bodies' (Katz, 2000, p 135). In contrast, the second group is stoic older adults, who embody the values of rural culture like self-reliance, practicality and the importance of hard work and religion (Dorfman et al, 2004).

These two groups are contrasted because they exemplify the diversity element of the best-fit model. Community active and stoic older adults have quite different experiences of ageing even while living in the same rural community. They have a penchant for different activities and respond in their own ways to the available natural, human-built and social resources of the community in which they live. Thus they experience different sets of resources as age-friendly. Stoic older persons may experience their community as age-friendly because they know where to go for goods and services and are surrounded by longstanding neighbours and friends. In contrast, for community active older adults, salient community features might be access to active outdoor recreation, to volunteer work or to opportunities to nurture their broad social networks.

The natural, human-built and social resources that constitute age-friendly rural communities for community active older adults are not the same as for stoic older adults (Table 11.1). Differences between the two groups are illustrated through the voices of older adults, augmented by interviews with family members, service providers and community leaders. In total, 149 individual interviews and 10 focus groups were completed. Data reported here were gathered through community case studies in three different rural communities in Canada: a seasonal community in Nova Scotia, a retirement community in Ontario and a farming community in Alberta (see Eales et al, 2006, for a full description of these communities).

Natural environment: the fit for older adults

Stoic and community active older people relate differently to the natural environment. A rural community is age-friendly for stoic older people as long as their surroundings are clean, quiet and naturally beautiful: "Two things that are very important, I think, is that [the community] is a lovely clean town to live in. And the second thing is the scenery around here is just out of this world"; "[Community] is becoming known as a peaceful, quiet, beautiful town surrounded by the salt water".

Table 11.1: Age-friendly rural communities: the 'best-fit' approach

Resources of rural communities	Groups of older adults	
	Stoic	*Community active*
Natural environment • good air/water quality • climate and topography	Age-friendly communities occur when stoic older people: • live in a clean, quiet setting • have opportunities to relate to the natural environment through productive activities of farming, gardening, etc	Age-friendly communities occur when community active older people: • have opportunities to interact with nature through walking, hunting, fishing, etc
Human-built environment • housing • stores/services • barrier-free spaces • transportation	Age-friendly communities occur when stoic older people: • are able to live in their own homes • are close to adequate basic and health services that they need as they grow older • are able to drive to obtain basic necessities nearby Having a barrier-free environment is not salient to stoic older persons	Age-friendly communities occur when community active older people: • have options for more supportive housing as their needs change • have stores/services that are available, although not necessarily proximate as long as they have the resources to access services at a distance • are able to drive to facilitate their own social engagement, or that of others in the community; distance is not a hindrance Having a barrier-free environment is not salient to community active older people

continued

Resources of rural communities	Groups of older adults	
	Stoic	*Community active*
Social environment • availability of family and friends • inclusive opportunities for engagement • activities that promote well-being	Age-friendly communities occur when stoic older people: • are proximate to family, close friends and good neighbours – familiar people with whom they can interact in the course of their everyday routines Opportunities to be engaged socially and participate in community organisations and events are not salient as stoic older people have little interest in community participation	Age-friendly communities occur when community active older people: • have opportunities to be socially active, volunteer and keep busy without feeling stretched Proximity to family/ friends is not salient as community active older people have the resources to maintain relationships, even across distances

Stoic older people often worked (or may even continue to work) in primary resource industries, such as farming or fishing, and they view the natural environment as a resource to nurture:

> 'The land here is forever. The people come and go. And I would like to leave the land in a little better condition and in better, more productive [state] than I found it, when I started it. Which I think I've been doing. I'm happy with that.'

While the natural environment constitutes the work environment of stoic older people, it is the playground of community active older people. For community active older people, age-friendly communities offer opportunities for outdoor leisure activities, such as walking, hunting and playing golf: "[The community] area, the whole area's absolutely beautiful. A beautiful place to live with the beaches at your fingertips"; "My husband ... he's a hunter, he's a fisherman, and he plays a lot of golf.... So [the community] offers him a lot too as a retirement [place]".

Human-built environment: the fit for older adults

The experience of rural communities also differs for stoic and community active older people because of the different ways in which they relate to resources in the human–built environment: housing, stores and services, transportation and barrier-free spaces.

A rural community is age-friendly for stoic older people as long as they can continue to live in their own homes. Stoic older people enjoy the comfort and security of their own home and familiar surroundings. They see themselves as ageing-in-place, "stay[ing] in my own house, thank you". The idea of moving to perhaps more appropriate housing as their needs change does not appeal to them at all: "With luck I'll drop dead before I have to [move]".

Community active older people also enjoy their homes and would like to continue living there. Yet they are cognisant of the limitations of their homes as they grow older. Some make plans to find more appropriate housing, while others undertake structural renovations to make their homes more accessible. Still others consider leaving because they cannot find more appropriate housing locally:

> 'After [my husband] died I stayed there two years, and then I bought a house in town.... It was a problem, maintaining the property and I did get help.... And I had a wheelchair ramp built in the garage ... and I had a wall cut in the living room, a door cut in the living room, and it was just a two-way ramp there.'

> 'Our health is very good for our age, but it's breaking down bit by bit. We have a fairly nice home.... What we've been looking around at is getting into a place where you don't have to cook.... The place where we really went to ... was [in a larger city 59 kilometres away].... It's a place where you get your meals. It's very, very nice.... But then you ... look at the price. It's $36,000 a year for the two of us.... You want to think about how much money you have left and how much time you have left. Is now the time to blow it on good living?'

For stoic older people, a rural community is age-friendly only if the goods and services that they need are available locally. They make few demands on stores and services and generally are content with what is available locally, sometimes to their detriment. They may do without a needed service rather than leave the familiarity of their community to access these services elsewhere.

> 'I am definitely not strong enough to drive out of town to get prescriptions. And if I can't get [medications] here, I'll go without.... Now I don't have [a] doctor ... [but] I find everything perfect, [community is] perfect, as far as it goes, yup.'

Unlike stoic older people, a rural community is age-friendly for community active older people if it is within reasonable driving distance of larger centres that offer more varied and specialised goods and services. They often keep a list of the items that they need from larger urban centres. One family member described her mother's 'city list' as: "Groceries that she can't get here, certain margarines, certain meats, certain fruits … clothing necessities…. She can't even buy her good pens here…. Good pens that have got a good senior grip". They recognise the limited availability of local services, and access desired services in other communities, some at a great distance:

> 'I was very fortunate that I got in to the doctor in [a larger town, 28 kilometres north] because there's still quite a [waiting] list there. And [this larger town] is not too bad of a drive…. It isn't really any different than driving to [another larger town, 36 kilometres south]. I mean, it's not a problem for me to drive at all.'

> 'We have theatre tickets in [city 200 kilometres away], seasons tickets, so we go out of the village for entertainment, but a lot of our entertainment comes from just getting together for dinner with friends and having them in and going out.'

Transportation and the ability to drive is salient to the age-friendliness of rural communities for both stoic and community active older adults. However, the purpose behind their driving differs. Stoic older people perceive driving as a sign of their independence: "I would be lost if I could not drive around town". Public transportation is often unavailable in rural areas in Canada (see Chapter Nine, this volume), so stoic older people rely on their vehicles to access needed supplies and services in their community: "No, we have no transportation. There are no buses any more. We have a car, though. Can't be without a car in this country really".

While stoic older people talk about driving as a means of meeting material needs, community active older people use their vehicles to support their social relationships and civic engagement: "I have a friend that has never driven a car and I'm her wheels"; "I was driving for Cancer [volunteer programme that transports people requiring cancer treatment] for four or five years".

> 'We've gone down [to the large city, 200 kilometres away] with a car and gone out for dinner and we've parked out of town and taken the Go train or subway…. And occasionally there's something at the Academy Theatre in [another city, 36 kilometres away] and we go to see that, sometimes as a group. We'll drive or if there's really a big group, we've even taken a bus there and gone out for dinner.'

> 'I drive this old lady, a 97-year-old, to church every Sunday. She lives down the road here. You know, we just drive them [older adults] places … and see that they get to the teas and the luncheons.'

Having interior and exterior spaces that are barrier-free is generally not salient for either stoic or community active older people. These older adults may not mention issues of accessibility because for them it is not a criterion for fit. However, having interior and exterior spaces that are barrier-free and enabling may be important in determining 'fit' for other older adults who have a physical disability or mobility challenges. As one service provider commented,

> 'We still have our stores that only have stairs that you couldn't get in there if you had a walker or a wheelchair.... Our post office is wheelchair accessible, our grocery store's wheelchair accessible. Our healthcare centre is wheelchair accessible. So the places that would be very commonly used [by older adults] are wheelchair accessible. But again, you wouldn't want to be going out on the street here in a wheelchair, or even a walker, in the winter. Summer, sure, not a problem, but in the winter, you wouldn't be going very far.'

Social environment: the fit for older adults

The experience of rural communities also differs for stoic and community active older people because of the divergent ways in which they relate to resources in the social environment, particularly family, friends and community organisations.

Akin to resources in the human-built environment, people also need to be proximate because stoic older people do not reach out. They are familiar with people, but not intimate in their social relationships. They become connected to others through their work or chance meetings in the course of their daily routines:

> 'In a small town your friends are the people you say hello to at the post office every morning, or the daycare centre if you happen to be there, and that ... you've known them all your lives and it's nice to have them around, even though perhaps I don't see them that often, or interact with them that often, they're always there, and you know they're always there.'

There has to be a close enough connection so that stoic older people will even ask for assistance. In many cases, only ongoing proximity creates the link that provides opportunities to ask for help.

> 'If you need help ... or anything, they're [her neighbours are] right there to help you. I don't bother my neighbours, I don't. I'm not one to go to this house, that house. I go to the Smiths', that's the only one I really go to.'

For community active older people, any rural community might be age-friendly as long as they can maintain their social connections to friends and family members. Effort is made to sustain ties to those nearby and at a distance: "He doesn't drink the coffee here, but [he] pay[s] $1.25 just to be with the men"; "My kids are very important to me. We spend a lot of time going back and forth [between provinces]".

Having an abundance of places and programmes for active leisure and socialisation does not contribute to stoic older people's experience of age-friendly rural communities. They have little interest in participating in community activities and events, preferring solitary leisure activities: "I do not go and golf and I do not curl. I do not belong to the Legion. I do not belong to the seniors' centre association and I don't want to"; "I have time to read lots.... Playing at cards and those things are just a waste of time".

Neither availability of nor access to social amenities seems to make a difference to stoic older people's participation: "They have a good, good active seniors' rec centre and club there. So a lot of people enjoy that. But I'd rather read my old magazines here at home"; "I can pretty well always get a ride [to cards] … but a lot of the time, I didn't – well, I just didn't feel like bothering".

In contrast, opportunities for active leisure and socialisation are vitally important to community active older people's experiences of age-friendly rural communities. They participate extensively in community programmes, organisations and events.

> 'Yesterday morning I went over to the Auxiliary [nursing home] in the morning. I go every Monday morning to help … from there I went directly over to the seniors' centre and we had some students from the high school come over and help us decorate.... Tomorrow I have to make a cake for the church to take to the funeral tomorrow afternoon'.

> 'I don't have to be satisfied with just belonging to the Legion, I'm a Mason, I can join the Lion's club, I can go to a seniors' club, you know. There's plenty for me to do.'

Community active older people believe that it is important to be engaged in their community for both personal and social reasons. They are fond of their community and want to contribute. Community involvement gives them a sense of accomplishment and a feeling of security. By investing their time and effort into community service, they believe they are making their community a better place to live: "One of the things that's really important for seniors is to be viewed as useful"; "[Older adults are] the movers and the shakers. They get the stuff done in this community"; "If you want to live in a certain type of community, you have to make a contribution to making it that kind of community.... And to get involved is the way to do that".

Conclusion

The natural, human-built and social resources of a community make a difference to whether rural settings are good places to grow old. Yet characteristics of 'place' are important, as Sherry Ann Chapman and Sheila Peace illustrate so eloquently in Chapter Three. However, they are not the sole determinants of whether communities are supportive. Older adults and their ways of interacting with these resources are also important. The question that needs to be asked is: what features of communities are age-friendly for which groups of older people?

Those who are stoic need communities that are structured to meet their basic needs and facilitate their social connections with others. The local availability of human-built resources is important to the maintenance of stoic older adults' everyday lives as is the spatial configuration of the community itself. It is primarily through their patterns of daily life that stoic older people become known in the community. Individuals who live near stoic older people or work in places they frequent, such as the bank, post office, grocery store or pharmacy, become familiar and part of an 'implicit monitoring system' (Rowles, 1998, p 111). Planning communities with neighbourhoods and core service centres that foster social interaction may contribute to the age-friendliness of communities for stoic older adults. Also, programmes targeting service providers to heighten their awareness of the diversity among older adults and their needs may be of benefit.

In comparison, those older adults who are actively engaged in their communities have more agency in effecting the fit. They use their resources of time, skill, money and health to foster the best fit between their personal preferences and environmental resources, including going beyond the physical boundaries of their community to obtain goods and services or nurture relationships. Yet agency has its limits. Some community active older adults reside in rural communities with few resources and are drawn into over-extending themselves through high levels of volunteerism. For them, an age-friendly community would be a place that fosters civic engagement without conscripting older adults through compulsory volunteerism.

Our research challenges normative conventions that there can be one model or guide to developing an age-friendly community. 'Fit' is dynamic; it varies depending on the personal preferences and resources of older adults and those of their communities at a particular point in time. Governments and community planners need to consider the ways in which the older people in their midst interact, and adjust their approaches accordingly. Congruence may be improved through adaptation by older adults, by communities, or by both. Context matters.

TWELVE

Revisiting rural ageing

Norah Keating

Introduction

Throughout this book, authors have undertaken analyses of processes of ageing in rural contexts. A goal has been to deconstruct unidimensional although opposing constructs of rural places as 'hinterlands bereft of opportunity and socially and culturally lagging or of idyllic pastoral settings' (Chapter One, p 1). Rural settings explored in this book are diverse. Older adults in South-East England and those in the vast prairies of western Canada live in places that differ considerably in size, distance from services and landscape. Such rural places represent both hinterlands and idyllic settings – and yet neither of these. Authors have addressed many such stereotypes of older adults and of rural places, expanding discourses about ageing in rural settings. Lifecourse and critical human ecology approaches have been used to situate older adults across time and in relation to place.

While processes of ageing are often acknowledged, understanding ageing requires a lifecourse perspective where change is assumed and interrogated. Authors have examined change across the adult lifecourse through longitudinal research on the evolution of convoys of support from family and friends; through comparisons of community participation of people across the adult lifespan; and through narratives of older adults looking forward towards the next phases of their lives and backward as they reflect on the ongoing creation of their identities as they traverse the lifecourse. These examinations of ageing put the focus on the unfolding of lives rather than on the more usual emphasis on late-life resources and frailties.

Critical reflections in this book are about the interaction between these processes of ageing of rural adults and the contexts of their lives: space, place, people and time. Authors have explored diversity by considering a variety of older adults. In their work, we see stark contrasts between active, engaged older adults who comprise the core of the voluntary sector in their communities, and those who are excluded by lack of material resources and poor social relationships.

In this final chapter, main sets of findings are explored: about rural places and beliefs; about processes of ageing; and about the 'best fit' between these places and processes and the contexts in which rural people grow older.

Understanding rural places and beliefs

In the exploration of ageing in rural settings, a key issue has been to consider conceptualisations of rural that are most relevant in understanding whether rural settings are good *places* to grow old. In Chapter One, Norah Keating and Judith Phillips describe 'type of locality' definitions, which are based on sociospatial elements of places including population size, density and distance from larger urban centres. They note that such definitions have been criticised as atheoretical since they lack a critical analysis of why spatial features of place might structure rural life. Nonetheless, approaches to understanding rural are often used by governments to highlight what are seen as particular needs of rural people. There are strongly held beliefs that place does influence rural life.

In several chapters, authors have undertaken this critical exploration of rural places, illustrating how such features might indeed structure the lives of older adults. For example, Neena Chappell et al (Chapter Six) provide a striking image of remote communities where caregivers live in tiny settlements, hundreds of kilometres away from service centres, with no public places in which to gather. Such isolation means that caregivers must wait several months and pay high prices for supplies and equipment necessary to support those for whom they care. In remote communities, some older adults have no electricity or running water, making personal and end-of-life care particularly difficult. Lack of public places in these communities precludes opportunities to gather to discuss issues of mutual concern. For them, community size and geographic isolation, combined with severe winter climate, have a profound influence on the ways in which care is provided.

Characteristics of rural places also influence the ways in which people become engaged in their communities. Because of their small size and distance from larger centres, rural communities often have few human resources and a tenuous service infrastructure from which to provide services and support to others. Rural residents respond by engaging in volunteer activities and community organisations at higher rates than urban dwellers. They do so despite chronic health problems and disabilities, even when this engagement places high demands on their own time, money and physical resources. Julia Rozanova et al (Chapter Eight) have shown that physical aspects of communities make a difference in people's behaviour. Those in remote communities provide more help to family members and friends especially in communities that are rapidly ageing, with low population density, and declining populations. Lower rates of volunteering are associated with community characteristics such as a higher proportion of people who are visible minorities that inhibit inclusion of residents into organisations. Higher rates are associated with community characteristics that foster the emergence and development of volunteer organisations and opportunities such as a higher proportion of older adults and of highly educated people.

Small, scattered populations and distance also influence employment environments. For people who deliver in-home services such as homecare, employment costs are high. Long distances between clients and inadequate rural infrastructure including poor roads, add to wear and tear on vehicles, and increased costs in petrol, insurance and repairs. Unreliable mobile phone connections and poor winter driving conditions increase personal safety risks (Joanie Sims-Gould and Anne Martin-Matthews, Chapter Five).

These various explorations of the impact of rural localities on the lives of rural residents show that rural locality makes a difference. Population size and dispersion influence work patterns of community service providers, resources available to family/friend caregivers and patterns of participation of older adults. Together, they build a convincing argument that rural ageing is 'place and space dependent' (Tamara Daly and Gordon Grant, Chapter Two).

Evidence presented in this book also points to the connections between rural places and the beliefs and behaviour of those who live there. It is at the interface between these sociocultural elements of rural, and the place-based characteristics of rural communities, that we gain a deeper understanding of the 'constructed' as well as the structural elements of rural. For example, Sherry Ann Chapman and Sheila Peace (Chapter Three) show how the physicality of rural landscapes is reflected in the narratives of rural women whose connections to the land are essential parts of their identities.

Others have explored the linkages between personal beliefs and patterns of behaviour distinctive of rural residents. Janet Fast and Jenny de Jong Gierveld (Chapter Seven) address the assumption that rural communities foster participation of rural residents because of volunteer opportunities that draw them in. They provide evidence that people *believe* that small rural settings allow them to do things that they would not be able to do in a larger place, which would require a higher level of knowledge or skill. They also believe that their assistance is needed by their communities. Compared with urban residents, rural adults of all ages had higher levels of volunteering, helping others and belonging to community organisations. It seems likely that these distinctive patterns of participation stem from beliefs that community engagement is both necessary and possible.

Similarly, Joanie Sims-Gould and Anne Martin-Matthews (Chapter Five) show how client–worker relationships are constructed by rural home support workers. From their research, we see how small, stable communities that foster close relationships among residents require workers to manage their professional roles while providing service to people with whom they have longstanding relationships. In these rural settings, the personal 'trumps' the more distant professional relationship. Workers believe they cannot opt out of picking up a few groceries for their clients or checking in on them on the weekend, or they feel badly if they do set such boundaries. Here too rural settings interact with beliefs and the behaviour of rural residents in relation to one another.

Collectively, we have moved towards addressing previous discourse about definitions of rural being atheoretical and unidimensional. Authors have helped deconstruct singular notions of rural as location or of a particular set of beliefs. Working at the interface of rural places and beliefs, authors have traced pathways between space, beliefs and behaviour, building the case for the validity of exploring rural ageing.

Understanding rural ageing

The expanded understanding of processes of rural ageing developed throughout the book provides a basis for evaluation of whether rural settings are good places to *grow* old. Lifecourse constructs of time have been used extensively to frame discussions of ageing and to bring attention to pathways towards old age. Chapters in this book include reports of rural ageing based on prospective studies of the evolution of support networks of adults; cohort analyses of adults from their twenties to their eighties and older; and narratives of older adults of their pathways to later life and their expectations of very old age. These processes and related continuities and discontinuities have added to our knowledge about ageing in rural settings and to the heterogeneity of people in late life.

Time is a fundamental construct in lifecourse theory. Time has many facets that bring different elements of ageing into focus. Among these, two have been featured in our explorations of rural ageing. Biological time helps us understand how physical processes of ageing influence lifestyles, community participation and social networks of adults as they age. The concept of 'natural' time has been important in understanding environmental patterns that shape rhythms of life. Latitude, seasonality and patterns of daylight and darkness are elements of these rhythms. To a lesser extent, we have used a third element – historic time – to consider how events shape experiences of cohorts of people now in advanced age, and how events with longlasting significance such as wars or economic depression can influence the evolution of rural communities.

Physical changes with age underlie discussions in many of the chapters, illustrating how processes of biological time are important in the lives of adults growing older in rural settings. A point made at various places in the book is that ageing is a normative process. While the likelihood of chronic illness increases with age, ageing is not inevitably related to ill-health or frailty. Janet Fast and Jenny de Jong Gierveld (Chapter Seven) provide an example of the intersections of age, chronic health and disability in their cohort analysis of adults from age 25 onwards. They found lower rates of participation among people with chronic health problems at all stages of the adult lifecycle. These results underline the importance of disentangling age and disability in our understanding of constraints and opportunities available to rural residents as they grow older.

Critical turning points can arise as a result of normative processes of ageing. In Chapter Nine, Bonnie Dobbs and Laurel Strain trace the impact of changes in driving status. They illustrate how older rural adults may decide not to drive for a number of reasons including normative age-related changes such as reduced night vision. Among older drivers there are lower proportions of older women compared with older men. The current cohort of older women is at higher risk of cumulative effects of turning points across the adult lifecycle, including being widowed. For them, widowhood may increase the likelihood of being without access to a car since many have relied on their husbands to drive them.

Normative physical changes in late life may also influence the ways in which older adults participate in their communities. Despite physical changes that accompany old age, evidence presented here is that rates of participation in volunteering, community organisations and in helping others decline sharply only among people over age 75 (Fast and de Jong Gierveld, Chapter Seven). Yet community contributions that are less dependent on health and mobility are remarkably stable. For example, charitable donations do not drop off with age or chronic health problems. In fact, slightly higher proportions of those over age 75 with and without disabilities make donations. Such participation may be an example of how people maintain their community connections in the face of changes in their physical resources as they age.

Older rural adults think about the possibilities of the onset of chronic illness and whether their communities will have the services they may need to support them. Some anticipate leaving their communities should their health needs increase, while others choose to live with increased risk in order to stay in familiar settings (Eales et al, Chapter Eleven). The onset of chronic health problems can have a profound impact on interactions with community members, especially family and friends. Clare Wenger and Norah Keating (Chapter Four) trace the evolution of social networks of adults in their mid-sixties through their mid-eighties and older. They show that as care needs increase, support networks become smaller and more focused on close kin. Their findings suggest that we need to rethink the assumption that older adults in rural communities are embedded in broad networks of friends, neighbours and families who are available to provide support when needed.

Together, authors in this book have illustrated both normative and non-normative physical changes associated with ageing. In their critical analyses of the pathways towards old age they have shown how these pathways are diverse. They have challenged assumptions that frailty is inevitable. At the same time, they have shown that rural communities may not have the resources to provide high levels of support that are needed by some older adults who develop late-life chronic health problems.

A second concept of time – 'natural' time – is relevant to the experience of growing older in rural settings. The idea of natural time comes from the ways in which physical environments shape both long-term and immediate experiences and rhythms of life. For example, Sherry Anne Chapman and Sheila Peace (Chapter Three) show how in the prairie region of western Canada, lives of women have been shaped by broad sweeps of time across periods of drought as a result of relentless wind. There, the constant presence of harsh climate and dramatic seasonal changes bind people to the land through their farming work. Similarly, the more tranquil microenvironments of the English countryside and gardens are equally important in helping people retain a sense of themselves by overlooking green fields and through their ability to open the door and go into their garden.

In these northern settings, seasonal differences influence daily patterns of engagement with others. Chapman and Peace describe how in winter months, streets of English villages are dark, residents close their shutters and older adults feel isolated in their homes. Remote northern communities have even more dramatic seasonal differences. People live in virtual darkness throughout the winter and 'white nights' in summer. Such an environment highlights the need for respite for family/friend caregivers who are housebound by virtue of their caregiving responsibilities, darkness and extreme cold (see Chappell et al, Chapter Six).

All of the chapters in this book draw on experiences of older adults in the northern hemisphere. Thus, we cannot compare their experiences to those of older adults in environments with extreme heat and drought that may be equally challenging to those described here. There is much more to be learned about how rhythms of the natural environment influence processes of ageing.

Historic time provides a relevant backdrop to these other processes unfolding in the lives and communities of older rural adults. Events that changed the economic status of communities have longstanding effects on succeeding generations. Examples from mining communities in North Wales and fishing communities in eastern Canada are informative. In North Wales, some older adults in need of care have no proximate children to support them. Many of these communities have had longstanding patterns of out-migration of young people resulting from mine closures and lack of alternative employment. In eastern Canada, closure of shipbuilding and fishing industries has led to the withdrawal of other services and a similar decline in employment opportunities. A typical comment about these changes comes from a resident of a small coastal village. She bemoaned the fact that trains no longer stopped, coaches did not come and services were disappearing, summing up her views of community decline by remarking that one day soon even the tide would not come in. In such places, ageing of communities has resulted in fewer resources to support increasing proportions of older residents.

Authors have articulated processes of rural ageing at the intersection of these elements of time. Normative changes as well as anticipated chronic illness lead people to consider whether they will be able to stay in their communities. Along with physical ageing, support networks may become smaller and connections to community more tenuous. Yet overall rates of community participation remain high into late life. Broad sweeps of historic time change the face of rural communities. In some cases, communities have fewer resources just at the time when there are high proportions of older adults who would benefit from a vibrant community infrastructure. Rhythms of the natural environment shape rural identities in ways that have not yet been fully articulated in understanding ageing in rural communities.

Understanding the 'fit' between older adults and rural contexts

Enhanced understanding of rural places and of processes of ageing in rural communities has been accompanied by a third main theme. Understanding rural ageing requires thinking about people's relationships with the natural, human-built, social and community settings in which they grow older. The emphasis in this final section of the chapter is on new knowledge of the ways in which rural contexts may be *good* places in which to grow old.

Exploration of this question was informed by the critical human ecology concept of 'best fit'. People are assumed to have varying capacities to interact with and benefit from their environments. However, there is no a priori list of characteristics of people and settings that would be most supportive to older adults. What is important is the complementarity of resources of older adults and their communities. For those with high levels of personal resources such as good health, adequate income and ability to drive, small rural communities with few basic services can be supportive places in which to grow old. Such older adults have high levels of personal agency that allow them to purchase local goods and services regardless of cost, maintain contact with family and friends at a distance and use their social connections to help them maintain links to their communities.

Yet older adults experience their communities in a variety of ways. A 'good fit' is not inevitable – a point articulated by Thomas Scharf and Bernadette Bartlam (Chapter Ten) in their discussion of social exclusion. They note that in different parts of the Western world, 30%-40% of older rural adults report difficulty with access to services and that rural older people are less likely to receive social services than are those in cities. As a result of such limitations, rural communities may have features that lead to exclusion.

There are many examples of low levels of community resources among rural settings discussed in this book. Lack of formal services and difficult working environments for rural workers can result in people being unable to get access to basic services and in high turnover among rural professionals. Limitations of the built environment such as lack of street lighting and sidewalks and buildings that are not accessible can create disability. Communities in remote regions that also have unique language or customs may be doubly isolated by distance and problems with access to mainstream services.

Rural communities are not uniformly resource-poor. While many are experiencing decline, the numbers of well-resourced communities is growing. Retirement communities attract urban professionals because of their natural beauty, recreational opportunities, purpose-built housing and reasonable access to larger urban centres. Community features such as these can act as resources for older adults, enhancing participation in volunteering and other community activities. Yet some community features that foster participation would not usually be seen as resources. Julia Rozanova et al (Chapter Eight) found that declining population, limited economic diversity and low population density were associated with higher levels of community participation. It may be that residents in such settings have no alternative but to compensate for lack of community infrastructure by being volunteers and caregivers to others.

Further, particular community features may not be resources to all older rural residents. Jacquie Eales et al (Chapter Eleven) illustrate clear differences between 'community active' and 'stoic' older people in what makes communities age-friendly for them. Affordable local services are important to stoic older people who will forego goods or services rather than travel to other centres. Generally they expect little of their communities, so they feel well supported. In contrast, community active older people welcome volunteer opportunities that arise because of limited formal sector resources. They do not place high value on local services since they go to larger places where they have more choices in goods and services.

Some older adults fare poorly in communities that have low levels of resources and where their poverty and poor social connections create invisibility. For them, the small pool of people, and volunteer and caregiver fatigue because of such limited human resources, heightens their exclusion. Rural communities may be stretched to compensate for lack of personal resources of older adults living at the margins.

Personal resources make a difference in the likelihood that older adults will experience their communities as good places to grow old. Being able to drive a car and having the financial resources to do so provide access to a much broader area than the local community. Skills in forming new social relationships reduce the potential for isolation in rapidly changing communities with high levels of in-migration. These resources are the basis for 'agency' – the ability to connect with people and services that can enhance the fit between individuals and their communities.

In contrast, compromised personal resources are especially problematic when rural environments cannot provide appropriate accommodations. Tamara Daly and Gordon Grant (Chapter Two) point out that chronic health problems are not just biological states borne by individuals. Yet they become so in community settings that have limited formal resources and where family and friends and the voluntary sector experience caregiving fatigue because of high levels of responsibility for care. Communities with limited resources may not be in a position to provide the higher levels of support needed by those whose health is poor.

Individuals may also be excluded because their personal characteristics are not viewed as resources. For example, those who speak a different language or have a religion other than that of the majority may be excluded by virtue of their differences. An example of accommodating such individual characteristics comes from Chapter Six on respite for caregivers, where Neena Chappell et al found that in Inuit communities with specific cultural and language traditions, respite came not from community services but from spending time with others from the same cultural background. Visiting and having traditional foods such as tea and bannock were the ways in which they experienced a break from their caregiving responsibilities. 'Best fit' is achieved when communities are sensitive to individual resources, preferences, culture and language.

Our focus on processes of ageing has highlighted pathways to old age of people in rural settings. The continuities and discontinuities in their lives are reflected in changing levels of personal resources. As resources change, so too does the interface of individuals with their environments. Thus, 'best fit' is fluid, reflecting the interplay of various elements of time, self and social contexts.

Authors of this book have provided evidence of the ways that individuals, family members and communities respond to renegotiate the person–environment fit. Some older adults anticipate changes and plan for them. An example comes from Jacquie Eales et al (Chapter Eleven). Older adults who were managing well in their rural settings because of their high levels of personal resources, such as energy, ability to drive and purchasing power, looked ahead to a time when they might leave their communities if they needed chronic care. Others chose to live with less security because of increased risks of falls or lack of transportation in order to stay in the place in which they had become integrated (Chapman and Peace, Chapter Three). Some shift their community contributions from active volunteering to making donations in response to changing resources, energy levels and active community connections (Fast and de Jong Gierveld, Chapter Seven). Still others move short distances to be closer to services but remain part of the overall community. Best fit does not necessarily come from being in a place that has the most services or other supports. Sometimes 'best' is to live with risk but retain one's identity.

Changes in communities also require older adults to renegotiate community connections or leave their communities for more supportive settings. As Thomas Scharf and Bernadette Bartlam (Chapter Ten) have shown, places with high levels of social or economic change can lead to social isolation for people who have difficulty making new social connections. Communities in decline can be difficult places to grow old for all but the most resourceful older adults. Family members often fill gaps in services and help compensate for lost community resources. However, as Clare Wenger and Norah Keating (Chapter Four) have shown, they have limited abilities to shore up both declining health of their relatives and dwindling community services over long periods of time.

Conclusion

In sum, the answer to the question of whether rural communities are good places to grow old must be that 'it depends' – on people's place in the lifecourse, on the community settings in which they live and on the ways in which they construct their relationships to people and place. Diversity among rural settings and among older rural adults is immense. The challenges of ageing are highlighted in rural places because of the powerful impact on identities of rural people by natural environments, distance and climate. Rural places are both idyllic and difficult just as older rural adults are both resilient and fragile. The journey through the deconstruction of stereotypes of rural ageing undertaken by the authors in this book has resulted in a richer understanding of ageing in rural settings.

References

Aartsen, M., Van Tilburg, T., Smits, C. and Knipscheer, K. (2004) 'A longitudinal study of the impact of physical and cognitive decline on the personal network in old age', *Journal of Social and Personal Relationships*, vol 21, no 2, pp 249-66.

Achenbaum, W.A. (1997) 'Critical gerontology', in A. Jamieson, S. Harper and C. Victor (eds) *Critical approaches to ageing and later life*, Buckingham: Open University Press, pp 16-26.

ACSA (Aged and Community Services Australia) and NRHA (National Rural Health Alliance) (2004) *Older people and aged care in rural, regional and remote Australia: A discussion paper*, Melbourne: ACSA and NRHA.

Ajrouch, K.J., Antonucci, T.C. and Janevic, M.R. (2005) 'Social networks among blacks and whites: the interaction between race and age', *Journal of Gerontology: Social Sciences*, vol 56B, no 2, pp S112-S118.

AlbertaFirst.com (2007) *Oyen population*, retrieved 23 April 2007 from www.albertafirst.com/profiles/statspack/20447.html

Alberta Tourism (2007) *Alberta Canada travel and tourism guide*, retrieved 15 April 2007 from www.albertatourism.com/

Allen, C.D. (1997) 'Women with physical disabilities: lifecourse strategies and perspectives', PhD dissertation, University of New Mexico, Albuquerque, NM.

Alston, M. (2007) 'Globalisation, rural restructuring and health service delivery in Australia: policy failure and the role of social work?', *Health and Social Care in the Community*, vol 15, no 3, pp 195-202.

Anderson, M., Helms, L.B., Black, S. and Myers, D.K. (2000) 'A rural perspective on home care communication about elderly patients after discharge', *Western Journal of Nursing Research*, vol 22, no 2, pp 225-43.

Andrews, G. and Phillips, D. (2005) 'Geographical studies in ageing: progress and connections to social gerontology', in G. Andrews and D. Phillips (eds) *Ageing and place: Perspectives, policy, practice*, London: Routledge, pp 7-13.

Antonucci, T., Lansford, J., Schaberg, L., Baltes, M., Takahashi, K., Smith, J., Akiyama, H., Fuhrer, R. and Dartigues, J. (2001) 'Widowhood and illness: a comparison of social network characteristics in France, Germany, Japan, and the United States', *Psychology and Aging*, vol 16, no 4, pp 655-65.

Arcury, T.A., Preisser, J.S., Gesler, W.M. and Powers, J.M. (2005a) 'Access to transportation and health care utilization in a rural region', *Journal of Rural Health*, vol 21, no 1, pp 31-8.

Arcury, T.A., Quandt, S.A., Bell, R.A., McDonald, J. and Vitolins, M.Z. (1998) 'Barriers to nutritional well-being for rural elders: community experts' perceptions', *Gerontologist*, vol 38, no 4, pp 490-8.

Arcury,T.A., Gesler,W.M., Preisser,J.S., Sherman,J., Spencer,J. and Perin,J. (2005b) 'Special populations, special services: the effects of geography and spatial behavior on health care utilization among the residents of a rural region', *Health Services Research*, vol 40, no 1, pp 135-55.

Armstrong, P. and Kits, O. (2001) *One hundred years of caregiving*, Report commissioned by the Law Commission of Canada, Ottawa, ON.

Atchley, R. (1999) *Continuity and adaptation in aging: Creating positive experiences*, Baltimore, MD: Johns Hopkins University Press.

Atkin, C. (2003) 'Rural communities: human and symbolic capital development, fields apart', *Compare: A Journal of Comparative Education*, vol 33, no 4, pp 507-18.

Bailey, L. (2004) *Aging Americans: Stranded without options*, Washington, DC: Surface Transportation Policy Project.

Baltes, M. and Carstensen, L.L. (1996) 'The process of successful ageing', *Ageing and Society*, vol 16, no 4, pp 397-422.

Barber, J. (1998) 'Rural disadvantage in the distribution of south Australian home and community care funding', *Australian Journal of Social Issues*, vol 33, no 3, pp 231-9.

Barham, C. and Begum, N. (2006) *The new urban/rural indicator in the Labour Force Survey*, London: Office for National Statistics, Labour Market Trends.

Barton, L. and Oliver, M. (eds) (1997) *Disability studies: Past, present and future*, Leeds: The Disability Press.

Bauman, Z. (1998) *Work, consumerism and the new poor*, Buckingham: Open University Press.

Bell, D. (1997) 'Anti-idyll: rural horror', in P. Cloke and J. Little (eds) *Contested countryside cultures: Otherness, marginalisation and rurality*, New York: Routledge, pp 94-108.

Bender, B. (1993) 'Introduction: landscape – meaning and action', in B. Bender (ed) *Landscape: Politics and perspectives*, Oxford: Berg, pp 1-17.

Bengtson, V.L. and Allen, K.R. (1993) 'The life course perspective applied to families over time', in P.G. Boss, W.J. Doherty, R. LaRossa, W.R. Schumm and S.K. Steinmetz (eds) *Sourcebook of family theories and methods: A contextual approach*, New York: Plenum Press, pp 469-99.

Bennett, D.G. (1996) 'Implications of retirement development in high-amenity nonmetropolitan coastal areas', *Journal of Applied Gerontology*, vol 15, pp 345-60.

Bernard, M. and Phillips, J. (1998) *The social policy of old age*, London: Centre for Policy on Ageing.

Bernard, M. and Phillips, J. (2000) 'The challenge of ageing in tomorrow's Britain', *Ageing and Society*, vol 20, no 1, pp 33-54.

Bernard, M., Phillips, J., Machin, L. and Harding Davies, V. (eds) (2000) *Women ageing: Changing identities, challenging myths*, London: Routledge.

Beshiri, R. (2004) 'Immigrants in rural Canada: 2001 update', *Rural and Small Town Canada Analysis Bulletin*, vol 5, no 4, p 27.

Bess, I. (1999) 'Seniors behind the wheel', *Canadian Social Trends*, vol Fall, no 54, pp 2-7.

Bevan, M. and Croucher, K. (2006) 'Delivering services for older people in rural areas', in P. Lowe and L. Speakman (eds) *The ageing countryside: The growing older population of rural England*, London: Age Concern England, pp 147-63.

Beverly Foundation and AAA Foundation for Traffic Safety (2004) *Supplemental transportation programs for seniors: A report on STPs in America*, Pasadena, CA.

Billig, M. (2004) 'Supportive communities, an optimum arrangement for the older population?', *Journal of Sociology and Social Welfare*, vol 31, no 3, pp 131-51.

Bourke, L., Sheridan, C., Russell, U., Jones, G., DeWitt, D. and Liaw, S.-T. (2004) 'Developing a conceptual understanding of rural health practice', *Australian Journal of Rural Health*, vol 12, no 5, pp 181-6.

Brandstadter, J. and Grieve, W. (1994) 'The aging self: stabilising and protective processes', *Developmental Review*, vol 14, pp 52-80.

Brody, E.M., Hoffman, C., Kleban, M.H. and Schoonover, C.B. (1989) 'Caregiving daughters and their local siblings: perceptions, strains, and interactions', *Gerontologist*, vol 29, pp 529-38.

Broese van Groenou, M. (2007) 'Deelname aan activiteiten' ['Participating in activities'], in T. van Tilburg and J. de Jong Gierveld (eds) *Zicht op eenzaamheid: Achtergronden, oorzaken en aanpak* [*Loneliness: Concept, causes and coping*], Assen, The Netherlands: Van Gorcum, pp 59-64.

Broese van Groenou, M., Glaser, K., Tomassini, C. and Jacobs, T. (2006) 'Socio-economic status differences in older people's use of informal and formal help: a comparison of four European countries', *Ageing and Society*, vol 26, pp 745-66.

Bronfenbrenner, U. (1994) 'Ecological models of human development', in T. Husen and T.N. Poslethwaite (eds) *International encyclopedia of education* (2nd edn, vol 3), New York: Elsevier Science, pp 1643-7.

Bronstein, L., McCallion, P. and Kramer, E. (2006) 'Developing an ageing prepared community: collaboration among counties, consumers, professionals and organizations', *Journal of Gerontological Social Work*, vol 48, pp 193-202.

Brown, D.M. and Stommes, E.S. (2004) 'Rural governments face public transportation challenges and opportunities', *Amber Waves*, February, retrieved 12 May 2007 from www.ers.usda.gov/amberwaves/February04/Findings/RuralGovernments.htm

Bubolz, M.M. and Sontag, M.S. (1993) 'Human ecology theory', in P.G. Boss, W.J. Doherty, R. LaRossa, W.R. Schumm and S.K. Steinmetz (eds) *Sourcebook of family theories and methods. A contextual approach*, New York: Plenum, pp 419-48.

Bull, N. (1998) 'Aging in rural communities', *National Forum*, vol 78, no 2, pp 38-42.

Burchardt, T., Le Grand, J. and Piachaud, D. (2002) 'Degrees of exclusion: developing a dynamic, multidimensional measure', in J. Hills, J. Le Grand and D. Piachaud (eds) *Understanding social exclusion*, Oxford: Oxford University Press, pp 30-43.

Bury, M. (1995) 'Aging, gender and sociological theory', in S. Arber and J. Ginn (eds) *Connecting gender and aging: A sociological approach*, Philadelphia, PA: Open University Press, pp 15-29.

Canadian Homecare Association (2006) *The delivery of home care services in rural and remote communities in Canada*, retrieved 30 July 2006 from www.cdnhomecare.ca/index.php

Carp, F.M. (1988) 'Significance of mobility for the well-being of the elderly', in Committee for the Study on Improving Mobility and Safety for Older Persons (ed) *Transportation in an aging society* (2nd edn), Washington, DC: Transportation Research Board, pp 3-20.

Cattan, M. (2002) *Supporting older people to overcome social isolation and loneliness*, London: Help the Aged.

Cavanaugh, C.A. (1997) '"No place for a woman": engendering western Canadian settlement', *The Western Historical Quarterly*, vol 28, no 4, pp 493-518.

Chapman, S.A. (2005) 'Theorizing about aging well: constructing a narrative', *Canadian Journal on Aging*, vol 24, no 1, pp 9-18.

Chappell, N.L. (1998) 'Maintaining and enhancing independence and well-being in old age', *Canada health action: Building on the legacy: Determinants of health, adults and seniors*, vol 2, Ottawa, ON: National Forum on Health, pp 89-137.

Chappell, N.L., Reid, C. and Dow, E. (2001) 'Respite reconsidered a typology of meanings based on the caregiver's point of view', *Journal of Aging Studies*, vol 15, pp 201-16.

CIESIN (Center for International Earth Science Information Network), Columbia University, IFPRI (International Food Policy Research Institute), The World Bank and CIAT (Centro Internacional de Agricultura Tropical) (2005) *Global Rural–Urban Mapping Project (GRUMP), Alpha Version*, Palisades, NY: Socioeconomic Data and Applications Center (SEDAC), Columbia University, retrieved 3 May 2007 from http://sedac.ciesin.columbia.edu/gpw/

CIHI (Canadian Institute for Health Information) (2006) *How healthy are rural Canadians? An assessment of their health status and health determinants*, Ottawa, ON: CIHI.

Clausen, J.A. (1998) 'Life reviews and life stories', in J.Z. Giele and G.H. Elder (eds) *Methods of life course research: Qualitative and quantitative approaches*, Thousand Oaks, CA: Sage Publications, pp 189-212.

Cloke, P., Milbourne, P. and Thomas, C. (1997) 'Living lives in different ways? Deprivation, marginalization and changing lifestyles in rural England', *Transactions of the Institute of British Geographers*, vol 22, no 2, pp 210-30.

Cohen, S. (2004) 'Social relationships and health', *American Psychologist*, vol 59, no 8, pp 676-84.

Coleman, P. (1997) 'The last scene of all', *Generations Review*, vol 7, no 1, pp 2-5.

Commins, P. (2004) 'Poverty and social exclusion in rural areas: characteristics, processes and research issues', *Sociologia Ruralis*, vol 44, no 1, pp 60-75.

Commission for Rural Communities (2007a) *Defining rural England*, CRC 49, Cheltenham: Commission for Rural Communities.

Commission for Rural Communities (2007b) *Views on the interim statement by the Commission on Integration and Cohesion*, Cheltenham: Commission for Rural Communities (www.ruralcommunities.org.uk).

Cornman, J., Lynch, S., Goldman, N., Weinstein, M. and Hui-Sheng, L. (2004) 'Stability and change in the perceived social support of older Taiwanese adults', *Journals of Gerontology Series B: Psychological Sciences and Social Sciences*, vol 59B, no 6, pp S350-S357.

Countryside Agency (2002) *Indicators of poverty and social exclusion in rural England*, Cheltenham: Countryside Agency.

Countryside Agency (2003) *Older people in rural England*, Research Note, Cheltenham: Countryside Agency.

Countryside Agency/Age Concern (2005) *Rural lifelines*, London: Age Concern England.

Cox, C. (1998) 'The experience of respite: meeting the needs of African American and white caregivers in a statewide program', *Journal of Gerontological Social Work*, vol 30, no 3/4, pp 59-72.

Cranswick, K. (2003) *General Social Survey Cycle 16: Caring for an aging society 2002*, Ottawa, ON: Statistics Canada.

Crosnoe, R. and Elder, G.H. (2002) 'Successful adaptation in the later years: a life course approach to aging', *Social Psychology Quarterly*, vol 65, no 4, pp 309-28.

Dahms, F. and McComb, J. (1999) '"Counterurbanization", interaction and functional change in a rural amenity area – a Canadian example', *Journal of Rural Studies*, vol 15, no 2, pp 129-46.

Daly, T. (2003) 'The grassroots ceiling: the impact of state policy change on home support nonprofits in Ontario and in Waterloo Region – Wellington-Dufferin (1958-2001)', PhD dissertation, Department of Health Policy, Management and Evaluation, Faculty of Medicine, University of Toronto.

de Jong Gierveld, J. and Hagestad, G.N. (guest editors) (2006) 'Social integration in later life; special issue', *Research on Aging*, vol 28, no 6, pp 627-778.

de Jong Gierveld, J., van Tilburg, T. and Dykstra, P.A. (2006) 'Loneliness and social isolation', in A. Vangelisti and D. Perlman (eds) *Cambridge handbook of personal relationships*, Cambridge: Cambridge University Press, pp 485-500.

DEFRA (Department for the Environment, Food and Rural Affairs) (2004) *Rural strategy*, London: DEFRA.

Desrosiers, J., Noreau, L. and Rochette, A. (2004) 'Social participation of older adults in Quebec', *Aging Clinical and Experimental Research*, vol 16, no 5, pp 406-12.

Desrosiers, J., Bourbonnais, D., Noreau, L., Rochette, A., Bravo, G. and Bourget, A. (2005) 'Participation after stroke compared to normal aging', *Journal of Rehabilitation Medicine*, vol 7, no 6, pp 353-7.

Dobbs, B.M. (2005) *Medical conditions and driving: A review of the literature (1960-2000)*, catalogue #DOT HS 809 690, Washington, DC: US Department of Transportation, available at www.nhtsa.dot.gov/people/injury/research/Medical_Condition _Driving/pages/Sec1-Intro.htm

Dobbs, B.M., Dobbs, A.R. and Strain, L. (2005) 'Transportation in rural areas: an investigation into the differential effects of lack of transportation between younger and older adults', Presentation at the Sixth Conference of the Canadian Rural Health Research Society and the First Conference of the Canadian Society for Circumpolar Health, Quebec City, PQ, 27-29 October, available at www.aging.ualberta.ca

Dobbs, B.M., Swindle, J., Keating, N., Eales, J. and Keefe, J. (2004) *Caring contexts of rural seniors: Phase 2 technical report*, Submitted to Veterans Affairs Canada in partial fulfilment of PWGSC Contract #51019-017032/001/HAL, Edmonton, AB, available at www.hecol.ualberta.ca/rapp

Dorfman, L.T., Murty, S.A., Evans, R.J., Ingram, J.G. and Power, J.R. (2004) 'History and identity in the narratives of rural elders', *Journal of Ageing Studies*, vol 18, pp 187-203.

DWP (Department for Work and Pensions) (2005) *Opportunity age: Meeting the challenges of ageing in the 21st century*, Cm 6466i, London: The Stationery Office.

Eales, J., Keating, N., Rozanova, J., Bardick, A., Swindle, J., Bowles, R.T., Keefe, J. and Dobbs, B. (2006) *Caring contexts of rural seniors: A case study of diversity among older adults in rural communities: Phase 3 technical report*, Submitted to Veterans Affairs Canada in partial fulfilment of PWGSC Contract #51019-017032/001/HAL, Edmonton, AB, available at www.hecol.ualberta.ca/rapp

Eldar, R. and Burger, H. (2000) 'Rural aging – a global challenge', *Croatian Medical Journal*, vol 41, no 3, pp 348-50.

Elder, G. (1974) *Children of the great depression*, Chicago, IL: Chicago University Press.

Eley, D., Young, L., Shrapnel, M., Wilkinson, D., Baker, P. and Hegney, D. (2007) 'Medical students and rural general practitioners: congruent views on the reality of recruitment into rural medicine', *Australian Journal of Rural Health*, vol 15, no 1, pp 12-20.

Erlinghagen, M. and Hank, K. (2006) 'The participation of older Europeans in volunteer work', *Ageing and Society*, vol 26, pp 567-84.

Eyles, J. (1985) *Senses of place*, Warrington: Silverbrook Press.

Fast, J.E., Charchuk, M., Keating, N., Dosman, D. and Moran, L. (2006) *Participation, roles and contributions of seniors*, Ottawa, ON: Social Development Canada, Knowledge and Research Directorate.

Findlay, R. and Cartwright, C. (2002) *Social isolation and older people: A literature review*, Brisbane: Australasian Centre on Ageing, University of Queensland.

Fiori, K., Antonucci, T. and Cortina, K. (2006) 'Social network typologies and mental health among older adults', *Journals of Gerontology Series B: Psychological Sciences and Social Sciences*, vol 61, no 1, pp 25-32.

Foley, D.J., Heimovitz, H.K., Guralnik, J.M. and Brock, D.B. (2002) 'Driving life expectancy of persons aged 70 years and older in the United States', *American Journal of Public Health*, vol 92, no 8, pp 1284-9.

Forbes, D.A. and Janzen, B.L. (2004) 'Comparison of rural and urban users and non-users of home care in Canada', *Canadian Journal of Rural Medicine*, vol 9, no 4, pp 227-35.

Friedland, W.H. (2002) 'Agriculture and rurality: beginning the "final separation"?', *Rural Sociology*, vol 67, no 3, pp 350-71.

Garbarino, J. (1986) 'Where does social support fit into optimizing human development and preventing dysfunction?', *British Journal of Social Work*, vol 16, supplement, pp 23-37.

Gardiner, M., Sexton, R., Kearns, H. and Marshall, K. (2006) 'Impact of support initiatives on retaining rural general practitioners', *Australian Journal of Rural Health*, vol 14, no 5, pp 196-201.

Garland, J. and Chakraborti, N. (2006) '"Race", space and place', *Ethnicities*, vol 6, no 2, pp 159-77.

Garung, R., Taylor, S. and Sheeman, T. (2003) 'Accounting for changes in social support among married older adults: insights from the MacArthur studies of successful aging', *Psychology and Aging*, vol 18, no 3, pp 487-96.

Gee, E.M. (2000) 'Population and politics: voodoo demography, population aging, and Canadian social policy', in E.M. Gee and G.M. Gutman (eds) *The overselling of population ageing: Apocalyptic demography, intergenerational challenges, and social policy*, Don Mills, ON: Oxford University Press, pp 5-25.

Gething, L. (1997) 'Sources of double disadvantage for people with disabilities living in remote and rural areas of New South Wales, Australia', *Disability and Society*, vol 12, no 4, pp 513-31.

Giarchi, G.G. (2006a) 'Older people "on the edge" in the countrysides of Europe', *Social Policy and Administration*, vol 40, no 6, pp 705-21.

Giarchi, G.G. (2006b) 'Editorial introduction', *Social Policy and Administration*, vol 40, no 6, pp 571-8.

Giddens, A. (1991) *Modernity and self-identity: Self and society in the late modern age*, Cambridge: Polity Press.

Giele, J.Z. and Elder, G.H. (eds) (1998) *Methods of life course research: Qualitative and quantitative approaches*, Thousand Oaks, CA: Sage Publications.

Gilbert, A., Philip, L. and Shucksmith, M. (2006) 'Rich and poor in the countryside', in P. Lowe and L. Speakman (eds) *The ageing countryside: The growing older population of rural England*, London: Age Concern England, pp 69-93.

Gilmour, J.A. (2002) 'Dis/integrated care: family caregivers and in-hospital respite care', *Journal of Advanced Nursing*, vol 39, no 6, pp 546-53.

Glasgow, N. (1993) 'Poverty among rural elders: trends, context, and directions for policy', *Journal of Applied Gerontology*, vol 12, no 3, pp 302-19.

Glasgow, N. and Blakely, R.M. (2000) 'Older nonmetropolitan residents' evaluations of their transportation arrangements', *Journal of Applied Gerontology*, vol 19, no 1, pp 95-116.

Gottlieb, B.H. (1995) *Impact of day programs on family caregivers of persons with dementia*, Guelph, ON: Gerontology Research Centre and Psychology Department, University of Guelph.

Government of Manitoba (2007) *Gimli chosen for age-friendly rural/remote research project*, available at www.gov.mb.ca/chc/press/top/2007/02/2007-02-16-111000-1226.html

Gray, D., Shaw, J. and Farrington, J. (2006) 'Community transport, social capital, and social exclusion in rural areas', *Area*, vol 38, no 1, pp 89-98.

Halfacree, K.H. (1993) 'Locality and social representation: space, discourse and alternative definitions of the rural', *Journal of Rural Studies*, vol 9, no 1, pp 23-37.

Hall, M., McKeown, L. and Roberts, K. (2001) *Caring Canadians, involved Canadians: Highlights from the 2000 national survey of giving, volunteering and participating*, Ottawa, ON: Statistics Canada.

Hall, R. and Coyte, P. (2001) 'Determinants of home care utilization: who uses home care in Ontario?', *Canadian Journal on Aging*, vol 20, no 2, pp 175-92.

Hanlon, N. and Halseth, G. (2005) 'The greying of resource communities in northern British Columbia: implications for health care delivery in already-underserviced communities', *Canadian Geographer*, vol 49, no 1, pp 1-24.

Harding, A., Whitehead, P., Aslani, P. and Chen, T. (2006) 'Factors affecting the recruitment and retention of pharmacists to practice sites in rural and remote areas of New South Wales: a qualitative study', *Australian Journal of Rural Health*, vol 14, no 5, pp 214-18.

Hart, G.L., Larson, E.H. and Lishner, D.M. (2005) 'Rural definitions for health policy and research', *American Journal of Public Health*, vol 95, no 7, pp 1149-55.

Hatch, L.R. (2000) *Beyond gender differences: Adaptation to aging in life course perspective*, Society and Aging Series, Amityville, NY: Baywood Publishing Company.

Heather, B., Skillen, L., Young, J. and Vladicka, T. (2005) 'Women's gendered identities and the restructuring of rural Alberta', *Sociologia Ruralis*, vol 45, no 1/2, pp 86-97.

Heinz, W.R. and Kruger, H. (2001) 'Life course: innovations and challenges for social research', *Current Sociology*, vol 49, pp 29-45.

Herold, M., Gordon, T., Kaye, K., Brockie, E. and Fuller, T. (2002) *Rural transportation series no. 4: Elderly and disabled rural residents: A continuing transportation issue*, Ottawa, ON: Government of Canada.

Herzog, A., Ofstedal, M. and Wheeler, L. (2002) 'Social engagement and its relationship to health', *Clinics in Geriatrics Medicine*, vol 18, no 3, pp 593-609.

Hicks, J. and Allen, G. (1999) *A century of change: Trends in UK statistics since 1900*, House of Commons Research Paper 99/111, 21 December, Social and General Statistics Section, London: House of Commons Library.

Holstein, M.B. and Minkler, M. (2007) 'Critical gerontology: reflections for the 21st century', in M. Bernard and T. Scharf (eds) *Critical perspectives on ageing societies*, Bristol: The Policy Press, pp 13-26.

Home Care Sector Study Corporation (2003) *Canadian home care resources study: Synthesis report*, Ottawa, ON: Home Care Sector Study Corporation.

Hong, L. (2006) 'Rural older adults' access barriers to in-home and community-based services', *Social Work Research*, vol 30, no 2, pp 109-18.

Horton, M. (2005) 'Rural crisis, good practice and community development responses', *Community Development Journal*, vol 40, no 4, pp 425-32.

Hudson, B., Hardy, B., Henwood, M. and Wistow, G. (1997) 'Working across professional boundaries: primary health care and social care', *Public Money and Management*, October-December, pp 25-30.

Hughes, A. (1997) 'Rurality and "cultures of womanhood": domestic identities and moral order in village life', in P. Cloke and J. Little (eds) *Contested countryside cultures: Otherness, marginalisation and rurality*, New York: Routledge, pp 123-37.

Janicki, M.P. and Ansello, E.F. (2000) *Community supports for aging adults with lifelong disabilities*, Baltimore, MA: Paul H. Brooks.

Joseph, A.E. and Cloutier-Fisher, D. (2005) 'Ageing in rural communities: vulnerable people in vulnerable places', in G.A. Andrews and D.R. Phillips (eds) *Ageing and place: Perspectives, policy, practice*, Oxford: Routledge, pp 133-46.

Joseph, A.E. and Martin-Matthews, A. (1993) 'Growing old in aging communities', *Journal of Canadian Studies*, vol 28, no 1, pp 14-29.

Kahana, E., Lovegreen, L., Kahana, B. and Kahana, M. (2003) 'Person, environment, and person–environment fit as influences on residential satisfaction of elders', *Environment and Behavior*, vol 35, no 3, pp 434-53.

Katz, S. (2000) 'Busy bodies: activity, aging, and the management of everyday life', *Journal of Aging Studies*, vol 14, no 2, pp 135-52.

Kearns, R. and Gesler, W. (1998) 'Introduction', in R. Kearns and W. Gesler (eds) *Putting health into place: Landscape, identity and well-being*, Syracuse, NY: Syracuse University Press, pp 1-16.

Keating, N., Fast, J., Frederick, M., Cranswick, K. and Perrier, C. (1999) *Eldercare in Canada: Context, content and consequences*, Ottawa, ON: Statistics Canada.

Keating, N., Otfinowski, P., Wenger, G.C., Fast, J. and Derksen, L. (2003) 'Understanding the caring capacity of informal networks of frail seniors: a case for care networks', *Ageing and Society*, vol 23, no 1, pp 115-27.

Keefe, J., Fancey, P., Keating, N., Frederick, J., Eales, J. and Dobbs, B. (2004) *Caring contexts of rural seniors: Phase I technical report*, Submitted to Veterans Affairs Canada in partial fulfilment of PWGSC Contract #51019-017032/001/HAL, Edmonton, available at www.hecol.ualberta.ca/rapp

Kendig, H. (2003) 'Directions in environmental gerontology: a multidisciplinary field', *Gerontologist*, vol 43, no 5, pp 611-15.

Kent, R.M., Chandler, B.J. and Barnes, M.P. (2000) 'An epidemiological survey of the health needs of disabled people in a rural community', *Clinical Rehabilitation*, vol 14, pp 481-90.

Kloseck, M., Crilly, R.G. and Mannell, R.C. (2006) 'Involving the community elderly in the planning and provision of health services: predictors of volunteerism and leadership', *Canadian Journal on Aging*, vol 25, no 1, pp 77-91.

Koopman-Boyden, P.G., Baxendine, S. and Pool, I. (2006) *Fertility and ageing in urban and rural areas: Is location important for successful ageing in New Zealand?*, EWAS Working Paper Series, Working Paper 1, Hamilton: Population Studies Centre, University of Waikato.

Kostyniuk, L.P. and Shope, J.T. (2003) 'Driving and alternatives: older drivers in Michigan', *Journal of Safety Research*, vol 34, pp 407-14.

Lansford, J., Antonucci, T., Akiyama, H. and Takahashi, K. (2005) 'A quantitative and qualitative approach to social relationships and well-being in the United States and Japan', *Journal of Comparative Family Studies*, vol 36, no 1, pp 1-22.

Lashewicz, B., Manning, G., Hall, M. and Keating, N. (2007) 'Equity matters: doing fairness in the context of family caregiving', *Canadian Journal on Aging*, vol 26 (Suppl 1), pp 91-102.

Laws, G. (1997) 'Spatiality and age relations', in A. Jamieson, S. Harper and C. Victor (eds) *Critical approaches to ageing and later life*, Maidenhead: Open University Press, pp 90-100.

Lawton, M.P. (1977) 'The impact of the environment on ageing and behavior', in J.E. Birren and K.W. Schaie (eds) *Handbook of the psychology of ageing*, New York: Van Nostrand Reinhold, pp 276-301.

Lawton, M.P. (1999) 'Environmental taxonomy: generalizations from research with older adults', in S. Friedman and T. Wachs (eds) *Measuring environment across the lifespan*, Washington, DC: American Psychological Association, pp 91-124.

Le Mesurier, N. (2003) *The hidden store: Older people's contributions to rural communities*, London: Age Concern England.

Lee, C. and Russell, A. (2003) 'Effects of physical activity on emotional well-being among older Australian women: cross-sectional and longitudinal analyses', *Journal of Psychosomatic Research*, vol 54, pp 155-60.

Lee, H. and Cameron, M. (2004) 'Respite care for people with dementia and their carers', *Cochrane Database of Systematic Reviews*, issue 1, article no CD004396.

Little, J. and Austin, P. (1996) 'Women and the rural idyll', *Journal of Rural Studies*, vol 12, no 2, pp 101-11.

Litwin, H. (1995) 'The social networks of elderly immigrants: an analytic typology', *Journal of Aging Studies*, vol 9, pp 155-74.

Litwin, H. (2001) 'Social network type and morale in old age', *Gerontologist*, vol 41, no 4, pp 516-24.

Litwin, H. and Landau, R. (2000) 'Social network type and social support among the old-old', *Journal of Aging Studies*, vol 14, no 2, pp 213-28.

Liu, A.Q. and Besser, T. (2003) 'Social capital and participation in community improvement activities by elderly residents in small towns and rural communities', *Rural Sociology*, vol 68, no 3, pp 343-65.

Lowe, P. and Stephenson, M. (2002) *Demographic ageing and rural areas*, London: Age Concern England.

McClimont, B. and Grove, K. (2004) *Who cares now?*, Carshalton Beeches: United Kingdom Home Care Association Limited, retrieved 21 September 2006 from www.ukhca.co.uk/pdfs/whocaresnow.pdf

McCracken, M., Tsetso, K., Jean, B., Young, K., Huxter, D., Halseth, G. and Green, M. (2005) *Seniors in rural and remote Canada: Position paper*, Ottawa: Canadian Rural Partnership, Advisory Committee on Rural Issues.

McGrath, W.L., Mueller, M.M., Brown, C., Teitelman, J. and Watts, J. (2000) 'Caregivers of persons with Alzheimer's disease: an exploratory study of occupational performance and respite', *Physical and Occupational Therapy in Geriatrics*, vol 18, no 2, pp 51-69.

McGrath, P., Patton, M.A., McGrath, Z., Ogilvie, K., Rayner, R. and Holewa, H. (2006) '"It's very difficult to get respite out here at the moment": Australian findings on end-of-life care for indigenous people', *Health and Social Care in the Community*, vol 14, no 2, pp 147-55.

McNally, S. (1999) 'The effects of respite care on informal carers' well-being: a systematic review', *Disability and Rehabilitation*, vol 21, pp 1-14.

McPherson, B. (2004) *Aging as a social process: Canadian perspectives*, Don Mills, ON: Oxford University Press.

Mahmood, A. and Martin-Matthews, A. (2008) 'Dynamics of carework: boundary management and relationship issues for home support workers and elderly clients', in A. Martin-Matthews and J.E. Phillips (eds) *Blurring boundaries: Ageing at the intersection of work and home life*, New York: Lawrence Erlbaum Associates, pp 21-42.

Manthorpe, J., Malin, N. and Stubbs, H. (2004) 'Older people's views on rural life: a study of three villages', *International Journal of Older People Nursing*, vol 13, no 6, pp 97-104.

Marshall, J. (1999) *Voluntary activity and the state: Commentary and review of the literature relating to the role and impact of government involvement in rural communities in Canada*, Report prepared for the New Rural Economy, Montreal, QC: Department of Sociology and Anthropology, Concordia University.

Martel, L. and Malenfant, É. (2007) *Portrait of the Canadian population in 2006 by age and sex: Findings*, Ottawa, ON: Statistics Canada.

Martin-Matthews, A. (2007) 'Situating "home" at the nexus of the public and private spheres: aging, gender and home support work in Canada', *Current Sociology*, vol 55, no 3, pp 229-49.

Martinson, M. and Minkler, M. (2006) 'Civic engagement and older adults: a critical perspective', *Gerontologist*, vol 46, pp 318-24.

Masotti, P.J., Fick, R., Johnson-Masotti, A. and MacLeod, S. (2006) 'Healthy naturally occurring retirement communities: a low-cost approach to facilitating healthy ageing', *American Journal of Public Health*, vol 96, no 7, pp 1164-70.

Mayer, K.U. (2000) 'Promises fulfilled? A review of 20 years of life course research', *Archives of European Sociology*, vol 41, pp 259-82.

Mead, N. and Bower, P. (2000) 'Patient-centredness: a conceptual framework and review of the literature', *Social Science and Medicine*, vol 51, pp 1087-110.

Melkas, T. and Jylhä, M. (1996) 'Social network characteristics and social network types among elderly people in Finland', in H. Litwin (ed) *The social networks of older people: A cross-national analysis*, Westport, CT: Praeger, pp 99-116.

Menec, V.H. (2003) 'The relation between everyday activities and successful aging: a 6-year longitudinal study', *Journal of Gerontology: Social Sciences*, vol 58B, pp S74-S82.

Merwin, E., Snyder, A. and Katz, E. (2006) 'Differential access to quality rural healthcare: professional and policy challenges', *Family and Community Health*, vol 29, no 3, pp 186-94.

Metz, D. (2003) 'Transport policy for an ageing population', *Transport Reviews*, vol 23, no 4, pp 375-86.

Milbourne, P. (2004) *Rural poverty: Marginalisation and exclusion in Britain and the United States*, London: Routledge.

Millar, W.J. (1999) 'Older drivers-a complex public health issue', *Health Reports*, vol 11, no 2, pp 59-71.

Miller, G.E. (2004) 'Frontier masculinity in the oil industry: the experience of women engineers', *Gender Work and Organization*, vol 11, no 1, pp 47-73.

Mills, M. (2000) 'Providing space for time: the impact of temporality on life course research', *Time and Society*, vol 9, no 1, pp 91-127.

Minore, B. and Boone, M. (2002) 'Realizing potential: improving interdisciplinary professional/paraprofessional health care teams in Canada's northern aboriginal communities through education', *Journal of Interprofessional Care*, vol 16, no 2, pp 139-47.

Morgan, D.G., Semchuk, K.M., Stewart, N.J. and D'Arcy, C. (2002) 'Rural families caring for a relative with dementia: barriers to use of formal services', *Social Science and Medicine*, vol 55, no 7, pp 1129-42.

Mugford, S. and Kendig, H. (1986) 'Social relations: networks and ties', in H.L. Kendig (ed) *Ageing and families: A social networks perspective*, Sydney: Allen and Unwin, pp 38-59.

Muilu, T. and Rusanan, J. (2004) 'Rural definitions and short-term dynamics in rural areas of Finland in 1989-97', *Environment and Planning A*, vol 36, pp 1499-516.

NAO (National Audit Office) (2002) *Tackling pensioner poverty: Encouraging take-up of entitlements*, Report by the Comptroller and Auditor General, HC 37 Session 2002-2003, 20 November, London: The Stationery Office.

Nemet, G.F. and Bailey, A.J. (2000) 'Distance and health care utilization among the rural elderly', *Social Science and Medicine*, vol 50, no 9, pp 1197-208.

Norman, A. (1985) *Triple jeopardy: Growing old in a second homeland*, Policy Studies in Ageing No 3, London: Centre for Policy on Ageing.

Northamptonshire County Council (2008) 'Mid year estimate 2004 Northamptonshire', retrieved 11 January 2008 from www.northamptonshire. gov.uk/democracy/council/census/census1.htm

OECD (Organisation for Economic Co-operation and Development) (2001) *Ageing and transport-mobility needs and safety issues*, Paris: OECD Publications Service.

Panelli, R. and Welch, R. (2005) 'Why community? Reading difference and singularity with community', *Environment and Planning A*, vol 37, no 9, pp 1589-611.

Pantazis, C., Gordon, D. and Levitas, R. (eds) (2006) *Poverty and social exclusion in Britain: The millennium survey*, Bristol: The Policy Press.

Parr, H., Philo, C. and Burns, N. (2004) 'Social geographies of rural mental health: experiencing inclusions and exclusions', *Transactions of the Institute of British Geographers*, vol 29, no 4, pp 401-19.

Patsios, D. (2006) 'Pensioners, poverty and social exclusion', in C. Pantazis, D. Gordon and R. Levitas (eds) *Poverty and social exclusion in Britain: The millennium survey*, Bristol: The Policy Press, pp 431-58.

Peace, S., Holland, C. and Kellaher, L. (2006) *Environment and identity in later life*, Maidenhead: Open University Press.

Perren, K., Arber, S. and Davidson, K. (2003) 'Men's organizational affiliations in later life: the influence of social class and marital status on informal group membership', *Ageing and Society*, vol 23, pp 69-82.

Peters, S. (1996) 'The politics of disability identity', in L. Barton (ed) *Disability and society: Emerging issues and insights*, London: Addison Wesley Longman, pp 215-34.

Philip, L. and Shucksmith, M. (2003) 'Conceptualising social exclusion in rural Britain', *European Planning Studies*, vol 11, no 4, pp 461-80.

Phillips, J.E. (1996) *Working and caring: Developments at the workplace for family carers of disabled and older people*, Dublin: European Foundation for the Improvement of Living and Working Conditions.

Phillips, J.E. (1999) 'The future of social work with older people in a changing world', in N. Parton (ed) *Social theory, social change and social work*, London: Routledge, pp 135-52.

Phillipson, C. and Scharf, T. (2005) 'Rural and urban perspectives on growing old: developing a new research agenda', *European Journal of Ageing*, vol 2, pp 67-75.

Phillipson, C. and Walker, A. (1986) *Ageing and social policy*, London: Gower.

Phillipson, C., Bernard, M., Phillips, J. and Ogg, J. (2000) *The family and community life of older people: Social networks and social support in three urban areas*, London: Routledge.

Pitkeathley, J. (2007) Keynote address, The Festival of International Conferences on Caregiving, Disability, Aging and Technology, 16-19 June, Toronto, ON, Canada.

Priestley, M. (2000) 'Adults only: disability, social policy and the life course', *Journal of Social Policy*, vol 29, no 3, pp 421-39.

Priestley, M. and Rabiee, P. (2002) 'Same difference? Older people's organizations and disability issues', *Disability and Society*, vol 17, no 6, pp 597-611.

Quarter, J., Mook, L. and Richmond, B.J. (2003) *What is the social economy?*, Research Bulletin of the Centre for Urban and Community Studies, Toronto, ON: University of Toronto.

Rajnovich, B., Keefe, J. and Fast, J. (2005) *Supporting caregivers of dependent adults in the 21st century: CPRN background paper*, Report prepared for the Healthy Balance Research Program, Halifax, NS: Canadian Policy Research Networks.

Reeve, D. (2002) 'Negotiating psycho-emotional dimensions of disability and their influence on identity constructions', *Disability and Society*, vol 17, no 5, pp 493-508.

Riley, M.W. and Foner, A. (1968-72) *Aging and society* (3 volumes), New York: Russell Sage.

Rioux, M. and Daly, T. (2006) 'Constructing disability and illness', in D. Raphael, T. Bryant and M. Rioux (eds) *Staying alive*, Toronto, ON: Canadian Scholar's Press, pp 305-24.

Rolland, J.S. (1994) *Families, illness and disability*, New York: Basic Books.

Rosenbloom, S. (2003) *The mobility needs of older Americans: Implications for transportation reauthorization*, Washington, DC: The Brookings Institution Series on Transportation Reform.

Rosenbloom, S. (2004) 'Mobility and the elderly: good news and bad', in Transportation Research Board, *Transportation in an aging society: A decade of experience*, Washington, DC: Transportation Research Board, pp 3-21.

Rothwell, N., Bollman, R.D., Tremblay, J. and Marshall, J. (2002) *Recent migration patterns in rural and small town Canada*, Agriculture and Rural Working Paper Series, Working Paper No 55, Ottawa, ON: Statistics Canada, retrieved 17 January 2007 from www.statcan.ca/english/research/21-601-MIE/21-601-MIE2002055.pdf

Rowles, G.D. (1983a) 'Geographical dimensions of social support in rural Appalachia', in G.D. Rowles and R.D. Ohta (eds) *Aging and milieu: Environmental perspectives on growing old*, New York: Academic Press, pp 111-30.

Rowles, G.D. (1983b) 'Place and personal identity in old age: observations from Appalachia', *Journal of Environmental Psychology*, vol 3, pp 299-313.

Rowles, G.D. (1998) 'Community and the local environment', in R.T. Coward and J.A. Krout (eds) *Ageing in rural settings: Life circumstances and distinctive features*, New York: Springer, pp 105-25.

Rowles, G.D. and Johansson, H.K. (1993) 'Persistent elderly poverty in rural Appalachia', *Journal of Applied Gerontology*, vol 12, no 3, pp 349-67.

Rowles, G.D. and Watkins, J.F. (2003) 'History, habit, heart and hearth: on making spaces into places', in K.W. Schaie, H.-W. Wahl, H. Mollenkopf and F. Oswald (eds) *Aging independently: Living arrangements and mobility*, New York: Springer, pp 77-96.

Rubenstein, R.L. and de Medeiros, K. (2004) 'Ecology and the aging self', in H.W. Wahl, R. Scheidt and P.G. Windley (eds) *Annual review of gerontology and geriatrics. Focus on aging in context: Socio-physical environments, vol 23*, New York: Springer Publishing Company, pp 59-84.

Rutter, M. (1996) 'Transitions and turning points in developmental psychopathology as applied to the age span between childhood and mid-adulthood', *International Journal of Behavioral Development*, vol 19, no 3, pp 603-26.

Salamon, S. (2003) 'From hometown to nontown: rural community effects of suburbanization', *Rural Sociology*, vol 68, no 1, pp 1-24.

Scharf, T. and Bartlam, B. (2006a) *Rural disadvantage: Quality of life and disadvantage amongst older people – a pilot study*, London: Commission for Rural Communities.

Scharf, T. and Bartlam, B. (2006b) *Quality of life and disadvantage among older people living in rural communities*, CRC 19, London: Commission for Rural Communities, available from www.ruralcommunities.gov.uk/publications/crc19

Scharf, T., Phillipson, C. and Smith, A. (2005a) *Multiple exclusion and quality of life amongst excluded older people in disadvantaged areas*, London: ODPM.

Scharf, T., Phillipson, C. and Smith, A. (2005b) 'Social exclusion of older people in deprived urban communities of England', *European Journal of Ageing*, vol 2, no 2, pp 76-87.

Scharf, T., Wenger, G.C., Thissen, F. and Burholt, V. (2005c) 'Older people in rural Europe: a comparative analysis', in D. Schmied (ed) *Winning and losing: The changing geography of Europe's rural areas*, Aldershot: Ashgate, pp 187-202.

Scheidt, R. and Norris-Baker, C. (2004) 'The general ecological model revisted: evolution, current status and continuing challenges', in H.W. Wahl, R. Scheidt and P.G. Windley (eds) *Annual review of gerontology and geriatrics: Focus on aging in context: Socio-physical environments, vol 23*, New York: Springer Publishing Company, pp 34-59.

Schindler, D.W. and Donahue, W.F. (2006) 'An impending water crisis in Canada's western prairie provinces', *Proceedings of the National Academy of Sciences of the United States of America*, vol 103, no 19, pp 7210-16.

Schuyt, T.N.M. and Gouwenberg, B.M. (2005) *Geven in Nederland 2005: Giften, legaten, sponsoring en vrijwilligerswerk* [*Giving in the Netherlands 2005: Gifts, bequests, sponsorships and volunteer work*], Den Haag, The Netherlands: Elsevier.

Scott, D.M., Newbold, K.B., Spinney, J.E.L., Mercado, R.G., Paez, A. and Kanaroglou, P.S. (2005) *Changing mobility of elderly urban Canadians, 1992-1998*, Hamilton, ON: Centre for Spatial Analysis, McMaster University.

Setterson Jr, R.A. (2003) *Invitation to the life course: Toward new understanding of later life*, Society and Aging Series, Amityville, NY: Baywood Publishing Company.

Shenk, D., Davis, B., Peacock, J.R. and Moore, L. (2002) 'Narratives and self-identity in later life: two rural American older women', *Journal of Aging Studies*, vol 16, no 4, pp 401-13.

Sherwood, K.B. and Lewis, G.J. (2000) 'Accessing health in a rural area: an evaluation of a voluntary medical transport scheme in the English Midlands', *Health and Place*, vol 6, pp 337-50.

Short, R. (2006) 'Boosting the immune system', *Nursing Older People*, vol 18, pp 18-21.

Shortall, S. (2004) 'Social or economic goals, civic inclusion or exclusion? An analysis of rural development theory and practice', *Sociologia Ruralis*, vol 44, no 1, pp 109-23.

Shucksmith, M. (2003) *Social exclusion in rural areas: A review of recent research*, London: Department for the Environment, Food and Rural Affairs.

Silverstein, M. and Parker, M. (2002) 'Leisure activities and quality of life among the oldest old in Sweden', *Research on Aging*, vol 24, pp 528-47.

Sims-Gould, J. and Martin-Matthews, A. (2007) 'Family caregiving or caregiving alone: who helps the helper?', *Canadian Journal on Aging*, Suppl 1, pp 27-46.

Smailes, P.J. (2002) 'From rural dilution to multifunctional countryside: some pointers to the future from South Australia', *Australian Geographer*, vol 33, no 1, pp 79-95.

Statistics Canada (2001) *A profile of the Canadian population by age and sex: Canada ages*, retrieved 17 January 2007 from www12.statcan.ca/english/census01/Products/Analytic/companion/age/subprovs.cfm#rural_and_small_town_areas

Statistics Canada (2003) *General Social Survey on social engagement*, Ottawa, ON: Statistics Canada.

Statistics Canada (2005a) 'Social relationships in rural and urban Canada', *The Daily*, 21 June 2005, retrieved 19 August 2007 from www.statcan.ca/Daily/English/050621/d050621b.htm

Statistics Canada (2005b) *Definitions and notes*, retrieved 19 August 2007 from www40.statcan.ca/l01/cst01/defdemo53a.htm

Statistics Canada (2006) 'Canada's population', *The Daily*, 21 December, retrieved 23 April 2007 from www.statcan.ca/Daily/English/061221/d061221d.htm

Statistics Canada (2007a) *Portrait of the Canadian population in 2006, by age and sex, 2006 Census*, catalogue no 97-551-XIE, Ottawa, ON: Statistics Canada.

Statistics Canada (2007b) 'More information on rural areas (RA)', in *2006 Census dictionary*, catalogue no 92-566-XWE, Ottawa, ON: Statistics Canada, retrieved 15 July 2007 from www12.statcan.ca/english/census06/reference/dictionary/geo042a.cfm

Stobert, S., Dosman, D. and Keating, N. (2005) *Aging well: Time use patterns of older Canadians*, Ottawa, ON: Statistics Canada.

Stockdale, A., Findlay, A. and Short, D. (2000) 'The repopulation of rural Scotland: opportunity and threat', *Journal of Rural Studies*, vol 16, pp 243-57.

Stoltz, P., Uden, G. and Willman, A. (2004) 'Support for family carers who care for an elderly person at home: a systematic literature review', *Scandinavian Journal of Caring Sciences*, vol 18, no 2, pp 111-19.

Stone, L. and Rosenthal, C. (1996) 'Profiles of the social networks of Canada's elderly: an analysis of 1990 General Social Survey data', in H. Litwin (ed) *The social networks of older people: A cross-national analysis*, Westport, CT: Praeger, pp 77-98.

Strang, V. and Haughey, M. (1999) 'Respite: a coping strategy for family caregivers', *Western Journal of Nursing Research*, vol 21, no 4, pp 450-71.

Strang, V.R. (2001) 'Family caregiver respite and leisure: a feminist perspective', *Scandinavian Journal of Caring Sciences*, vol 15, pp 74-81.

Strong-Boag, V. (1988) *The new day recalled: Lives of girls and women in English Canada, 1919-1939*, Markham, ON: Penguin Books.

Teitelman, J. and Watts, J. (2004) 'Family members' recommendations for achieving a mental break from caring for a loved one with Alzheimer's disease', *Alzheimer's Care Quarterly*, vol 5, no 3, pp 252-60.

Todd, S. and Shearn, J. (1996) 'Struggles with time: the careers of parents with adult sons and daughters with learning disabilities', *Disability and Society*, vol 11, no 3, pp 379-401.

Tornstam, L. (2005) *Gerotranscendence: A developmental theory of positive aging*, New York: Springer.

Townsend, P. (2007) 'Using human rights to defeat ageism: dealing with policy induced "structured dependency"', in M. Bernard and T. Scharf (eds) *Critical perspectives on ageing societies*, Bristol: The Policy Press, pp 27-44.

Tryssenaar, J. and Tremblay, M. (2002) 'Aging with a serious mental disability in rural Northern Ontario: family members' experiences', *Psychiatric Rehabilitation Journal*, vol 25, no 3, pp 255-64.

Turcotte, M. (2006) *Seniors access to transportation*, catalogue #11-008, Ottawa, ON: Statistics Canada.

Tyler, K. (2006) 'The impact of support received and support provision on changes in perceived social support among older adults', *International Journal of Aging and Human Development*, vol 62, no 1, pp 21-38.

UN (United Nations) (2001) *World urbanisation prospects: The 1999 revision*, New York: UN Population Division.

UN (2003) *International plan of action on ageing*, retrieved 1 December 2006 from www.un.org/esa/socdev/ageing/ageipaa.htm

Unger, J.B., Johnson, C.A. and Marks, G. (1997) 'Functional decline in the elderly: evidence for direct and stress-buffering protective effects of social interactions and physical activity', *Annals of Behavioral Medicine*, vol 19, pp 152-60.

Valdemarsson, M., Jernryd, E. and Iwarsson, S. (2005) 'Preferences and frequencies of visits to public facilities in old age – a pilot study in a Swedish town center', *Archives of Gerontology and Geriatrics*, vol 40, pp 15-28.

van Tilburg, T., de Jong Gierveld, J., Lecchini, L. and Marsiglia, D. (1998) 'Social integration and loneliness: a comparative study among older adults in the Netherlands and Tuscany, Italy', *Journal of Social and Personal Relationships*, vol 15, pp 740-54.

Vartanian, T.P. and McNamara, J.M. (2002) 'Older women in poverty: the impact of midlife factors', *Journal of Marriage and Family*, vol 64, no 2, pp 532-48.

Virnig, B., Moscovice, I., Durham, S.B. and Casey, M.M. (2004) 'Do rural elders have limited access to Medicare hospice services?', *Journal of the American Geriatrics Society*, vol 52, no 5, pp 731-5.

Wagner, C. (2006) 'Graying in rural England', *The Futurist*, vol 40, no 4, p 13.

Wahl, H.W. and Lang, F.R. (2004) 'Aging in context across the adult life course: integrating physical and social environmental research perspectives', in H.W. Wahl, R. Scheidt and P.G. Windley (eds) *Annual review of gerontology and geriatrics: Focus on aging in context: Socio-physical environments, vol 23*, New York: Springer, pp 1-33.

Wahl, H.W. and Weisman, G.D. (2003) 'Environmental gerontology at the beginning of the new millennium: reflections on its historical, empirical, and theoretical development', *Gerontologist*, vol 43, no 5, pp 616-27.

Walker, A. and Walker, C. (eds) (1997) *Britain divided: The growth of social exclusion in the 1980s and 1990s*, London: Child Poverty Action Group.

Watts, J. and Teitelman, J. (2005) 'Achieving a restorative mental break for family caregivers of persons with Alzheimer's disease', *Australian Occupational Therapy Journal*, vol 52, pp 282-92.

Wenger, G.C. (1989) 'Support networks in old age: constructing a typology', in M. Jefferys (ed) *Growing old in the 20th century*, London: Routledge, pp 166-85.

Wenger, G.C. (1990) 'Change and adaptation in informal networks of elderly people in Wales 1979-1987', *Journal of Aging Studies*, vol 4, pp 375-89.

Wenger, G.C. (1995) 'A comparison of rural and urban support networks: Liverpool and North Wales', *Ageing and Society*, vol 15, no 1, pp 59-81.

Wenger, G.C. (1997) 'Review of findings on support networks of older Europeans', *Journal of Cross-Cultural Gerontology*, vol 12, no 1, pp 1-21.

Wenger, G.C. (2001a) 'Intergenerational relationships in rural areas', *Ageing and Society*, vol 21, pp 537-45.

Wenger, G.C. (2001b) 'Myths and realities of ageing in rural Britain', *Ageing and Society*, vol 21, no 1, pp 117-30.

Wenger, G.C. and Scott, A. (1996) 'Change and stability in support network type: findings from a UK longitudinal study', in S. Formosa (ed) *Age vault: An INIA collaborating network anthology*, Malta: International Institute on Ageing, pp 105-20.

Wenger, G.C., Scott, A. and Seddon, D. (2002) 'The experience of caring for older people with dementia in a rural area: using services', *Aging and Mental Health*, vol 6, no 1, pp 30-8.

Wheeler, J.A., Gorey, K.M. and Greenblatt, B. (1998) 'Beneficial effects of volunteering for older volunteers and the people they serve: a meta-analysis', *International Journal of Aging and Human Development*, vol 47, pp 69-79.

WHO (World Health Organization) (2002) *Towards a common language for functioning, disability and health (ICF)*, Geneva: WHO, available from www.who. int/classifications/icf/en/

WHO (2006) *Global age-friendly cities project*, Geneva: WHO, available from www. phac-aspc.gc.ca/seniors-aines/pubs/age_friendly/index.htm

Wiebe, N. (2001) 'Rewriting the rural west', in R. Epp and D. Whitson (eds) *Writing off the rural west*, Edmonton, AB: University of Alberta Press, pp 325-30.

Williams, A. (1999) 'Place identity and therapeutic landscapes: the case of home care workers in a medically under serviced area', in A. Williams (ed) *Therapeutic landscapes: The dynamic between place and wellness*, Lanham, MD: University of America Press, pp 71-96.

Williams, A.M. and Cutchin, M.P. (2002) 'The rural context of health care provision', *Journal of Interprofessional Care*, vol 16, no 2, pp 107-15.

Williams, B. and Grant, G. (1998) 'Defining people-centredness: making the implicit explicit', *Health and Social Care in the Community*, vol 6, no 2, pp 84-94.

Wilson, J. (2000) 'Volunteering', *Annual Review of Sociology*, vol 26, pp 215-40.

Woods, M. (2005) *Rural geography*, London: Sage Publications.

Woods, M. (2006) 'Redefining the "rural question": the new "politics of the rural" and social policy', *Social Policy and Administration*, vol 40, no 6, pp 579-95.

Yoshino, S. (2006) *Older adults' care network typologies* [brochure], Edmonton, AB: University of Alberta, Hidden Costs/Invisible Contributions Research Program, available from www.hecol.ualberta.ca/hcic/publications/fact_sheets.htm

Zarit, S.H. (1998) 'Stress reduction for family caregivers: effects of adult day care use', *Journal of Gerontology: Social Sciences*, vol 53B, supplement, pp S267-S277.

Zerubavel, E. (1981) *Hidden rhythms: Schedules and calendars in social life*, Berkeley, CA: University of California Press.

Zingmark, K., Norberg, A. and Sandman, P.-O. (1995) 'The experience of being at home throughout the life span: investigation of persons from 2 to 102', *International Journal of Aging and Human Development*, vol 41, no 1, pp 47-62.

Index

A

Aartsen, M. 36, 42
age-friendly rural communities 109-10
  best-fit approach 112-13, 114-15
  resources approach 110-12
ageing 12, 121, 124-6, 129-30
  lifecourse perspectives 11-19
  see also older adults; population ageing
ageing well 21, 25-31
ageism 6-7
agency 4, 6, 128
  homecare 45, 48-9
  and lifecourse 11, 14-16
Alberta 23, 25, 28-9, 89-91
Allen, C.D. 18
Alston, M. 5
Amnesty International 66
Atchley, R. 15
Atkin, C. 35
attachment to place 21, 27-8
Australia
  policy environment 5
  remoteness 77-8
  rurality 2
  social exclusion 99
  support networks 35
autonomy 45, 50

B

Baltes, M. 15
Bangor Longitudinal Study of Ageing 37-42
Bartlam, Bernadette 3, 22, 35, 41
Bauman, Z. 97-8
beliefs 123
Bell, D. 23
Bennett, D.G. 111
best fit 4, 15, 112-20, 127-9
biological time 13, 124
Blakely, R.M. 90
Bourke, L. 2
Brandstadter, J. 15
Brasilia Declaration on Ageing iv
Brown, D.M. 91
Burton Latimer 23, 24, 29
Bury, M. 16, 18

C

calendars 14
Canada
  age-friendly rural communities 110, 113-20
  fishing communities 126
  homecare 43-51
  participation 65-75
  participation and community characteristics 77-86
  private vehicles 89-91

remoteness 77-8
respite 53-62
rurality 2, 22, 23
rurality and ageing well 21, 22, 23, 24-31, 125, 126
services 17, 110
social exclusion 99
social networks 5, 92-3
support networks 35-6, 42
visible minorities 84
care work 18
caregivers 53-6
Carp, F.M. 87-8, 92, 95
cars *see* private vehicles
Carstensen, L.L. 15
clocks 13
Cloutier-Fisher, D. 110
Coleman, P. 15-16
community 5
  and caregiver respite 59
  community active older adults 119
  exclusion from 100, 105-6, 107
  and mobility 88
  and participation 75-86
  rurality and ageing well 26-7, 31
  support networks 39-40
  and transportation 93-4
community active older adults 113-20, 128
community organisations 66, 69, 70, 72
compulsory volunteerism 61, 63, 73, 86, 120
continuity theory 15-16
cosmic time 13
critical gerontology 6-8, 100
critical human ecology 3-5
  see also best fit
Crosnoe, R. 15
cultural time 13-14
Cutchin, M.P. 50-1

D

Daly, T. 17
Desrosiers, J. 66
disability 12-13, 67, 124
  and access to private vehicles 91
  lifecourse perspectives 11-19
  and participation 63-73
distance
  homecare 44, 45-6
  respite 57
diverse networks 36
Dobbs, B.M. 92-3
donations 66, 70, 71, 72, 125

E

ecological perspective 44-9, 87-8
economic diversity 81
education 83-4

Elder, G. 19
Elder, G.H. 11, 15
employment 122-3
England
    rurality 23
    rurality and ageing well 21, 22, 23-4, 25-31,
        125, 126
    social exclusion 100-8
environments 4-5
    see also human-built environment; natural
        environment; social environment

F

family 36, 38, 40, 42, 53, 63, 103-4
    see also caregivers
Family Caregivers of Pictou County, Nova
    Scotia 56, 58
Finland 35, 36
Foner, A. 12
friends
    social networks 71-2
    support networks 36, 38-9, 63

G

Garbarino, J. 33
gender
    and access to private vehicles 90-1, 92
    and ageing 18
    see also men; women
General Social Survey on social engagement
    (Statistics Canada) 65, 77
Gething, L. 65
Giele, J.Z. 11
Gilmour, J.A. 55
Glasgow, N. 90
Global Age-Friendly Cities 109
Grieve, W. 15

H

Halfacree, K.H. 2
Hatch, L.R. 18
Haughey, M. 55
Heinz, W.R. 14-15
helping others 66, 69, 70, 72, 122
    and community characteristics 76, 78, 81, 82,
        83, 85, 86
historical time 13, 124, 126
homecare 43-51, 122-3
human agency *see* agency
human ecology
    assumptions 3-4
    and critical gerontology 6-8
human-built environment 111, 112, 113, 114,
    115-18

I

identity 16-19
independence 45, 50
institutional calendars 14

International Plan of Action on Ageing 109
interpersonal environment 5
    see also social environment
intersectionality 18-19
Inuit 56-7, 58, 59, 128-9
Ireland 98
Israel 35, 36

J

Joseph, A.E. 110

K

Keefe, J. 110
Kendig, H. 35
kin-keeping 27, 31
Kloseck, M. 64
Kruger, H. 14-15

L

Lang, F.R. 3-4
Laws, G. 6
Lawton, M.P. 110
Lewis, G.J. 51
lifecourse perspective 8, 11-19, 124
    older women 21, 24-5
linked lives 11, 12-13
Litwin, H. 36
locally integrated networks 36, 38-9, 40
location in time and space 11, 16-19

M

McGrath, W.L. 55
macroenvironments 4
Mayer, K.U. 19
membership in community organisations 66,
    69, 70, 72
men
    access to private vehicles 90-1, 92
    participation 77, 78, 79, 80, 82, 83, 84
Metz, D. 87
microenvironments 4
Mills, M. 13
mobility *see* transportation
Mugford, S. 35

N

natural environment
    age-friendly rural communities 110-11, 112,
        113, 114, 115
    rurality and ageing well 25-6, 31
natural time 13, 124, 125
Netherlands 36, 42
networks *see* social networks; support
    networks
New Zealand
    services 110
    social exclusion 99
Newfoundland and Labrador 56, 58
Norris-Baker, C. 5

North Wales *see* Wales
Northamptonshire 23-4
Nova Scotia 56

O

older adults iv
  age-friendly communities 109-20
  critical gerontology 6-8
  environments 4-5
  homecare 43-51
  mobility 87-95
  participation 63-73
  participation and community characteristics
    75-86
  rural areas 2-3, 22, 23-31, 127-9
  social exclusion 97-108
  support networks 33-42
  see also ageing
Opportunity age (Department for Work and
  Pensions) 98
othering 35, 41, 84
Oyen, Alberta 23, 25, 28-9

P

Panelli, R. 35
participation 63-73, 127-8
  and community characteristics 75-86
Pauktuutit Inuit Women of Canada 56-7, 58,
  59
Peace, S. 4
person–environment fit 4, 15, 112-20, 127-9
Peters, S. 18-19
Phillips, J.E. 7
physical environment 4
  see also human-built environment; natural
    environment
place 17
policy environment 5
population 79-80, 81-2
population ageing iv, v, 87
population change 105-6, 107, 108
population density 78-9
poverty 97-8, 99, 101-3, 107
privacy
  homecare 44-5, 46-8
  respite 57
private restricted networks 35-6, 38, 39, 40
private vehicles 88-90, 95, 124-5
  and personal resources 90-2
  social and community contexts 92-4
  and social exclusion 100, 105
psychological readiness 13

R

Reeve, D. 12
remoteness 56-8, 77-8, 122
resources approach 110-12
respite 53-62, 126, 128-9
Riley, M.W. 12

Rosenthal, C. 35-6
Rowles, G.D. 21
rural areas iv, 1-3, 22-3, 121, 122-4, 129-30
  age-friendly communities 109-20
  ageing, disability and participation 63, 65,
    67-73
  and ageing well 25-31
  best fit 127-9
  environments 4-5
  homecare 43-51
  lifecourse perspectives 11-19
  participation 63
  participation and community characteristics
    75-86
  respite 53-62
  social exclusion 97-108
  support networks 33-42
Rushton 23-4
Rutter, M. 19

S

Scharf, Thomas 3, 22, 35, 41, 110
Scheidt, R. 5
selective optimisation with compensation 15
self-sufficiency 99
  stoic older adults 113-20, 128
Seniors Resource Centre of Newfoundland
  and Labrador 56, 58, 59
services
  exclusion 99-100, 105, 107, 108
  homecare 43-51
  institutional calendars 14
  and remoteness 78
  respite 53-62
Setterson, R.A., Jr 16
Sherwood, K.B. 51
social constructions 2-3
social environment 111-12, 113, 114, 115,
  118-19
  see also interpersonal environment
social exclusion 76, 97-108
social integration 63, 64, 65, 71-2
  see also linked lives
social networks 33-4, 71-2
  exclusion 99, 103-4
  and mobility 88, 92-3, 95
social participation *see* participation
social time 13, 14
space 16-17
Stobert, S. 15
stoic older adults 99, 113-20, 128
Stommes, E.S. 91
Stone, L. 35-6
Strang, V.R. 55
Supplemental Transportation Programs for
  Seniors (STPs) 94
support networks 33-42, 125
  and social exclusion 103-4, 107
  see also caregivers

Sweden 111

T

time 11, 13-14, 124
transportation 28, 31, 78, 81, 87-95
  age-friendly rural communities 117
  homecare 44, 45-6, 51
  respite 57, 60
  and social exclusion 100, 105, 108
  and social networks 37
type of locality 2, 122

U

UK
  rural deprivation 98
  rurality 2, 22
  social exclusion 99, 100
  support networks 35, 36, 41
  see also England
United Nations 109
urban areas 65, 67-73
US
  rural deprivation 98
  support networks 35, 36
  transportation 94

V

vehicles *see* private vehicles
visible minorities 84
volunteering 63, 65-6, 67-9, 70, 72, 122
  age-friendly rural communities 120
  and community characteristics 76, 79-80, 81,
    82, 83-4, 85-6

W

Wahl, H.W. 3-4
Wales 29-30, 126
  support networks 37-42
Walker, A. 97
Walker, C. 97
Welch, R. 35
Wenger, G.C. 17, 37
Williams, A.M. 50-1
women
  access to private vehicles 90-1, 92
  participation 77, 79-80, 81, 82, 83-4, 85
  rurality and ageing well 21-31
World Health Organization (WHO) iv-v, 64,
    109-10

Critical Perspectives on Ageing Societies

*Edited by **Miriam Bernard** and **Thomas Scharf***

This important book brings together some of the best known international scholars working within a critical gerontology perspective to review and update our understanding of how the field has developed over the last twenty-five years and provide a challenging assessment of the complex practical and ethical issues facing older people, and those who conduct research on ageing, in the 21st century.

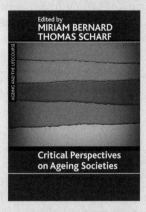

Edited by
MIRIAM BERNARD
THOMAS SCHARF

AGEING AND THE LIFECOURSE

Critical Perspectives on Ageing Societies

PB £24.99 US$39.95 **ISBN** 978 1 86134 890 6   240 x 172mm 200 pages May 2007
HB £65.00 US$99.00 **ISBN** 978 1 86134 891 3

Ageing in a Consumer Society
From passive to active consumption in Britain
Ian Rees Jones, Martin Hyde, Christina R Victor, Richard Wiggins, Chris Gilleard and Paul Higgs

This book provides a unique critical perspective on the changing nature of later life by examining the engagement of older people with consumer society in Britain since the 1960s. People retiring now are those who participated in the creation of the post-war consumer culture. These consumers

IAN REES JONES • MARTIN HYDE
CHRISTINA R VICTOR • RICHARD WIGGINS
CHRIS GILLEARD • PAUL HIGGS

AGEING AND THE LIFECOURSE

Ageing in a Consumer Society

From passive to active consumption in Britain

have grown older but have not stopped consuming; their choices and behaviour are products of the collective histories of both cohort and generation.

PB £24.99 US$39.95 **ISBN** 978 1 86134 882 1   240 x 172mm 256 pages tbc Sept 2008
HB £65.00 US$99.00 **ISBN** 978 1 86134 883 8

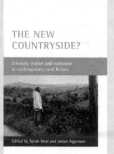